Managing Transformation Projects

Mark Kozak-Holland · Chris Procter

Managing Transformation Projects

Tracing Lessons from the Industrial to the Digital Revolution

palgrave
macmillan

Mark Kozak-Holland
Stouffville, ON, Canada

Chris Procter
Salford Business School
University of Salford
Salford, UK

ISBN 978-3-030-33037-8 ISBN 978-3-030-33035-4 (eBook)
https://doi.org/10.1007/978-3-030-33035-4

This Palgrave Pivot imprint is published by the registered company Springer Nature Switzerland AG
The registered company address is: Gewerbestrasse 11, 6330 Cham, Switzerland

Preface

Organisations are today facing a digital revolution that brings opportunities and threats, and are transitioning to new business models. Project management through transformational projects is playing a significant part in this revolution. This practice is largely conducted without reference to research or historical background. Indeed, this is indicative of a substantial gap between research and practice in project management more generally.

We examine the successful management of three nineteenth-century projects: namely the Stockton to Darlington Railway, the (U.S.) Transcontinental Railroad and the Manchester Ship Canal. These have been chosen because although each one commenced with the purpose of business optimisation, all three resulted in significant business transformation and disruption. In each case we show how the management of these projects led to their transformational impact.

The book demonstrates the relevance of these historical projects to contemporary digital transformation, and the vision and skills involved. In so doing it seeks to address the gap referred to above.

Stouffville, Canada
Salford, UK

Mark Kozak-Holland
Chris Procter

Acknowledgements The authors would like to acknowledge the support and assistance of Paul Spedding in reviewing the book.

About This Book

Themes

Project Management (PM), Business Transformation, Transformational Projects, Historical Case Studies, Megaprojects, Digital Revolution.

Scope

The book will provide evidence of the management of 3 projects from the nineteenth century which led to substantial business transformation. The lessons learnt are of great relevance to contemporary project management, particularly those concerned with disruptive technology.

Figures and Illustrations

Figures 3.1–3.3, 3 images from **John Weedy's Collection of Illustrated London News** as scanned and uploaded to the website:

https://www.iln.org.uk/iln_years/year/1864.htm.

Edition 1864, P393, Retrieved 23 May 2019

- Stephenson's locomotive manufactory at Newcastle upon Tyne October 15, 1864 P393—2 half page views of Stephenson's Locomotive factory at Newcastle upon Tyne: The Lathe and Tool shop and The fitting shop, and Steam Hammer.

Figures 3.4–3.5, 2 images from **Grace's Guide Collection** as scanned and uploaded to the website:

https://www.gracesguide.co.uk/.

(Original from University of Michigan)

Retrieved 23 May 2019

- Locomotion No. 1 opened the Stockton and Darlington Railway in 1825 (The Engineer, 1875)
- First Iron railway bridge, this is the bridge over the River Gaunless on the Stockton and Darlington Railway, designed by Robert Stephenson (The Engineer, 1875)
- The building of the Manchester Ship Canal 1889, Manchester Docks Section
- Ford at Trafford Park 1914, Ford installs first moving assembly line 1913.

Figures 4.1–4.3 images from Hathi Trust. Digital Library as scanned and uploaded to the website:

https://catalog.hathitrust.org/Record/000061498.

Rights: Public Domain.

Original from University of Michigan, the administrative host of HathiTrust, digitization program for the University of Michigan library.

Retrieved 27 May 2019

- Profile of the Pacific Railroad from Council Bluffs/Omaha to San Francisco. *Harper's Weekly* December 7, 1867, Drawn by C.H. Wells for Harper's Weekly December 7, 1867 (original engraving)
- Central Pacific Railroad, Chinese laborers at work (*Harper's Weekly* December 7, 1867)
- Completion of the Pacific Railroad—meeting of locomotives of the Union and Central Pacific lines: The engineers shake hands (*Harper's Weekly*, June 5, 1869, Photographed by Savage & Ottinger, Salt Lake City).

Contents

About the Authors

Dr. Mark Kozak-Holland 37-year career in IT has solely been in client facing projects. They have always involved solving client problems with solutions based on technology, process change or organisational adjustments. He has also completed extensive research into projects and their transformative effect on organisations. As a result, he is keenly aware of business transformation and how organisations can transition to a future digital end-state. Within his projects in a leadership and client consultative role he has helped organisations make the transition. Mark is also very passionate about history. In 2002 he founded the Lessons from History series to help today's business organisation find unique solutions to complex problems. The series uses relevant historical case studies to examine how historical projects and emerging technologies of the past solved complex problems. It then draws comparisons to challenges encountered in today's projects. As the lead editor behind the series he has brought together over a dozen authors with publications. He has written several academic papers on historical project management. He defended his dissertation titled The Relevance of Historical Project Lessons to Contemporary Business Practice to complete his Ph.D.

Dr. Chris Procter has been a project manager, lecturer, researcher and consultant in project management for over 30 years. He has significant experience in pedagogical research, which was the subject of his Ph.D., and professional development and practice. Chris has extensive experience as a lecturer at the University of Salford, UK, in teaching, researching and consulting on project management. He has won awards for his work on engaging students with the world of work and published widely on this. Effective learning and teaching should always be the product of a partnership with practice. The job of the academic is to reveal the relevance of the past to help students construct the future.

List of Figures

CHAPTER 1

The Challenge of Digital Transformation

Abstract Organisations are today facing a digital revolution that brings opportunities and threats, and are transitioning to new business models through projects, that can either transform or optimise. The authors propose that the digital revolution is just another industrial revolution driven by emerging technologies, like those in the past with the steam engine or electric dynamo/motor, but with greater impact to society. The right conditions for technology disruptions in an industry require three tipping points: emerging technology, culture through differing approaches to adoption, and regulations. Project management enables the transformation. Contemporary literature indicates that project failure is a major issue in digital transformation, partly because of the scale of transformations where a business has large numbers of systems and applications supporting its current operations.

Keywords Digital revolution · Digital business transformation or optimisation · Business processes · Opportunities and threats · Organisational resistance to change · Vision for digital customer journey · Leveraging of customer data · Iteration and agility

Living in a period of digital revolution leading to fundamental change of our lives, it is possible to forget that there have been previous periods of substantial business transformation, especially during the previous industrial

M. Kozak-Holland and C. Procter, *Managing Transformation Projects*, https://doi.org/10.1007/978-3-030-33035-4_1

revolutions. While we are familiar with contemporary digital disruption, for example in retail, logistics, service and many other sectors, we should not lose sight of the fact that previous generations have also experienced disruption.

Disruptive projects are not those that have optimised business processes: rather they are those that have changed or eliminated these very processes (Hammer and Champy 1993). We are not talking about projects that have improved CD quality when streaming is taking over, but those that have (for example) called into question the need for CDs in the first place. The success of Uber cannot be attributed to the provision of an improved taxi service but to a transformed approach to transport and logistics. The Stockton and Darlington Railway started as a quicker way to move coal across land to the sea but ended as a new way of transporting people between towns, and thence to major economic and social change in the UK and internationally. The Transcontinental Railroad reduced the time to cross the United States from 4 months to 4 days, and had a massive impact on the US economy. The Manchester Ship Canal, whose purpose was to optimise the transportation of goods from Manchester to the sea, led to the creation of the world's first industrial park leading to substantial disruption. These projects have been chosen as case studies for this book because each has in common (1) this change from optimisation to transformation (2) the role of project management in this change and (3) the volume of evidence available to us today. The fact that all three are concerned with transportation is not coincidental since changes to physical transport in the nineteenth century had a similar transformational impact to changes in digital 'transport' in the late twentieth/early twenty-first century.

The timing of such projects is vital, but their success is not due to luck or to vision alone. Behind all successful projects lies effective project management. Interestingly, however, academic analysis of what constitutes the effective management of these projects is very difficult to find. Even harder to find is any notion of the contemporary relevance of historical disruptive projects. It is our argument that there are significant lessons to be learnt from these projects from previous generations. The agility of projects from previous industrial revolutions is directly relevant to today's digital revolution. Project management is not a discipline that was founded in the twentieth century but a method of organisation that has evolved over thousands of years.

Furthermore, the analysis of contemporary business transformation is very limited in both the academic and professional press. Despite both the stunning successes and the substantial failure rate, the investigation of contemporary major disruptive projects is largely absent. The Project Management Bodies of Knowledge are dominated by process models, and the academic journals and programmes of study are dominated by operations management. The fundamental difference between project and operations management is that a project is by definition led by a temporary organisation which might subsequently change the established organisation's operations. Professional publications witness the digital revolution but provide little understanding.

The lessons of transformational projects do not fit within this discourse. Not only do transformational projects (in the words of the Agile Manifesto) 'respond to change rather than following a plan', they create the change. We believe that an analysis of transformational projects from the past can uncover how this came about. The digital revolution is just another industrial revolution driven by emerging technologies, like those in the past with the steam engine or electric dynamo/motor, but with possibly an even greater impact to society. While we do not set out to examine contemporary digital projects, this book can shine a light on the present and help to address the gap in our knowledge about the project management of the digital revolution.

The Difference Between Transformation and Optimisation

Organisations are today facing a digital revolution that brings opportunities and threats and are transitioning to new business models. Project management through transformational projects is playing a significant part in this revolution. This practice is largely conducted without reference to research or historical background. These projects are qualitatively different from projects aimed at optimisation or improvement.

According to Gartner (Prentice 2017):

> Digital business transformation is an effort to create connected platforms and new industry revenue streams. It is a type of digital journey that has the ambition of pursuing [completely] net-new revenue streams, product/services and business models. It is favoured by enterprises that must adapt to an industry in disruption, or ones that want to disrupt their industries.

Also from Gartner (Waller 2017):

> Business transformation is complicated, involving a constant tug-of-war between strategic vision and operational execution. One can't succeed without the other, yet few of us are comfortable in both camps. Digital business is a disruptive transformation that's not possible to achieve without the visionaries among us willing to push the boundaries of what's possible without sweating the details.

This is in contrast to digital business optimisation which is a type of digital journey that has the ambition of significantly improving existing business models through improved productivity, greater revenue generation of existing business streams and improved customer experience. It is favoured by enterprises whose industries are not going through disruption in the near term (LeHong 2017).

Based on these two definitions, some of the key characteristics of organisations undertaking these are:

1. Digital business transformation typically is led by start-ups, or newcomers (or those born digital first) that are driven by entrepreneurs. They are light on business processes, willing to take risks, make investments, innovate and explore technologies. According to Taneja (2019), Facebook's Mark Zuckerberg motto and often repeated mandate to his staff is 'Move fast and break'.
2. Digital business optimisation typically is led by existing organisations, traditional industry companies (or those born before the digital age) that are driven by competitive threats. They have a lot of business processes, and are less willing to take risk and make investments, constrained by process to innovate, explore technologies.

Established organisations that are late-comers to the digital age may be forced to change their business processes and models from ones designed to optimise the existing to those designed to explore and exploit the new. On the technology side, these changes will be substantial in the number of systems and applications to support in its current operations. Gartner Digital Business Survey (2018) finds 90% of traditional businesses are not yet transforming to digital business. Rather, they are pursuing digital optimisation, suggesting that the CIO and business leaders have not yet received board commitment to introduce new innovative digital products and services.

Right Conditions for Change

According to Gartner (Waller and Raskino 2017) technology disruptions in an industry have three tipping points: technology, culture and regulations.

> To take digital to the core of the business, CIOs, CEOs and digital strategists must track when culture, regulations and technology are ripe for innovation — the triple tipping point. Moving too soon or too late wastes money and harms the brand.

Technology provides the digital business opportunities. Optimum timing is based on ensuring the emerging technology is mature enough to be robust in operation and provide the business value to put ahead the company ahead of its competition. The company may have to innovate the technology to adapt it to the industry and create products that meet market needs. It is likely a combination of technologies is required where some of these could be highly specialised.

Cultural change can be highlighted by the differing approaches to the adoption of self-driving cars and according to Gartner (Waller and Raskino 2017):

> General Motors (GM) will invest $500 million in ride-sharing firm Lyft and develop autonomous vehicles where early cultural adoption will come more readily from ride-sharing services rather than car owners. By contrast, Volvo's IntelliSafe Autopilot marketing overcomes cultural barriers to adoption among individual car owners. Self-driving cars are too new for there to be a common point of view.

Regulations according to Gartner (Waller and Raskino 2017):

> More often, regulation will hold back digital business innovation; however, the lack of regulatory certainty also can be an enabler. New technology can be positioned in a way that circumvents existing regulation. In the early days of e-cigarettes, it wasn't clear whether they would be treated as a medical device or as tobacco. It wasn't clear whether laws designed to prevent smoking in offices would apply to vaping, and it wasn't clear how advertising rules applied.

Gartner recommends that all 3 are monitored and moved along, and this should be part of the overall strategy enabled by project management.

Digital Revolution Opportunities and Threats Examples

Gartner provides five examples primarily from traditional industry companies, not start-ups, which have exploited opportunities driven by the competitive threat of not responding to change in their industry:

1. 3M markets a Bluetooth-connected digital stethoscope that can send audio data to a PC for visual and algorithmic diagnostic analysis, or onward and over the Internet to a specialist. Usage of sensor information about physical asthma drug inhaling activity.
2. FedEx SenseAware tracks location and condition of a package through its journey as it sends out live updates about location and physical conditions (such as light and temperature).
3. Adidas markets a smart connected soccer ball with sensors that measure its speed, flightpath and spin. Data from the ball is transmitted to a smartphone or tablet via Bluetooth.
4. Allstate drones provide a safe and efficient way to inspect property damage quickly and remotely particularly important in large-scale natural disasters situations.
5. IKEA augmented reality catalog app helps customers try before they buy. It shows what items of furniture would look like in their own homes by overlaying a 3D rendering of a furniture item in correct proportion and perspective onto the live camera screen view of their living room or bedroom.

Other companies that have become digital giants include both traditional and start-ups. What they have in common is they have moved from pipelines, businesses which optimise their value chains to digital platforms, businesses that bring together consumers and producers and radically transformed their respective industry in creating new business models (Fig. 1.1).

Digital Transformation Failure

Contemporary literature indicates that project failure is a major issue in this context. According to Rogers (Forbes 2016) 84% of companies fail at digital transformation. According to KPMG's Global Transformation

Company	Current Business Model – pipeline business with value chain	Future Business Model – digital platform business
Youtube	Content Creator – Channel – Viewer	Content Creator – Platform – Consumer
Walmart	Supplier – Distributor - Distributor – Retailer – Consumer	Supplier – Walmart – Consumer
Amazon	Supplier – Distributor - Distributor – Retailer – Consumer	Supplier – Platform – Consumer
Uber	Taxi – Booking Office – Traveler	Taxi – Platform – Traveler
Airbnb	Didn't exist	Host – Platform – Traveler
Trivago	Host – Agent – Traveler	Host – Platform - Traveler

Fig. 1.1 Companies, typically new entrants, that have transformed themselves and their industries from a pipeline to a digital platform business model by using emerging technologies

Study (2016) less than half of the executives believe their initiatives will reach and maintain the value promised.

Examples of digital transformation failures are scant and under-reported for commercial reasons. However, examples of traditional companies in pole positions failing to transform include:

- Research In Motion (currently known as BlackBerry) could have disrupted itself by delivering BlackBerry Messenger and the BlackBerry network to iPhones and Android phones. While it would have given up exclusive use of these capabilities—thus disrupting itself—Research In Motion would have created market space within competitive ecosystems to grow its influence rather than watching it decline.
- Nokia, the world's dominant and pace-setting mobile-phone maker in 2007, was another significant failure, in a company that missed market and as a result was acquired by Microsoft (Surowiecki 2013). Historically, Nokia had been a surprisingly adaptive company, hardly a technological laggard. Nokia's development process was long dominated by hardware engineers who failed to recognize the increasing importance of software and also underestimated how important the transition to smartphones would be. Long after the iPhone's release Nokia insisted that its superior hardware designs would win over users.

Challenges Behind Digital Transformations

The scale of transformation can be daunting for even a mid-size business that typically has a large number of systems and applications to support in its current operations. Digital transformations need an organisation's Information Technology (IT) division or department to take a major role but often IT do not have the resources or influence to run major projects alongside the hundreds of smaller projects that are already in flight. A digital transformation requires a major consolidation of existing systems and applications invoking retire/replace strategies, and very demanding complex integration. This requires more IT resources and a focus shift to a more strategic and longer term view for applications that aligns to the changing world and new business strategies to cope with changes. According to Tiersky (2017), there are five top challenges that large enterprises, traditional companies, have when taking on transformation projects.

1. Organisational resistance to change—Tiersky (2017) points out that digital transformation, by its very nature, creates much chaos, but in times of change, not changing is far more risky:

   > The consequences of resistance to change manifests itself in a myriad of ways. Digital projects vital to a company's future success can have trouble getting funded, resourced, or marketed. These projects may be modified so as not to threaten retail or partner brands. They are held back by concerns about cannibalizing other revenue sources. They are asked to justify ROI to an unreasonable level of certainty. They are sent through endless legal reviews. Kodak invented the digital camera, but it was the internal resistance to change that led the company to bury it because it threatened the company's legacy film business.

   Further Morello (2016) advocates a need for a digital team to drive the digital transformation that is based on blends of the right behaviours (creatives, challengers, collaborators and co-operators) that constitute an ideal digital business sociology model.

2. Lack of a clear vision for a digital customer journey—(Tiersky 2017) points out that companies that succeed in creating a digital customer value proposition start by:

   > developing a clear vision of how they will meet their customers' digital needs, set objectives against that vision, and execute - often

over the course of multiple years. Often times, companies that are not succeeding simply haven't painted a clear picture of what they want – or need – to be when they digitally grow up. While clarifying this vision doesn't get you there by itself, in fact its only one of many steps, not having a vision is like going on a road trip without a destination. It's always possible you could stumble into something great, but probably not.

Further Burton et al. (2016) advocate a need for a digital platform strategy were CIOs collaborate with their business counterparts to integrate digital platform development into their technology and business strategic planning.

3. Ineffective gathering and leveraging of customer data—(Tiersky 2017) points out that the root of digital success is customer data:

> There's more to the tree than the root, to be sure, but whether it's Facebook, Amazon, Netflix or Uber, digital success stories have the effective gathering, storing and leveraging of customer data at the core. Many organisations today have a myriad of siloed systems containing various scraps of data about customer interactions, but no clear way to pull them together. Others have petabytes of data centralized in an information warehouse that they may use for reporting; however, they haven't figured out what to do with all that data in a manner that provides value to the customer.

Further Bloom (2019) highlights that collecting and unifying customer data is a tremendous technical challenge, with skills in short supply, and the single view of the customer has become more elusive, as well as less and less practical. CRM solutions contain plenty of valuable and verified customer information but lack the big data architecture needed to support the collection of real-time clickstream data from the web, mobile, and other digital channels.

4. Inflexible technology stack and development processes—(Tiersky 2017) point out that successful digital experiences are achieved through iteration and agility.

> Successful digital properties almost always iterate to success via the test and learn approach--where new features are being regularly added, measured, adjusted and pruned, based on user feedback and usage data. However, it is impossible to take this approach if your development process involves quarterly release cycles. Leveraging agile processes and

technologies that support frequent, if not continuous, integration and product releases are critical behaviours that lead to effective digital results.

5. Further Swanton et al. (2017) advocate a need to evolve current legacy IT platforms over time by integrating into a new digital business technology platform. This build as you go approach supports the new digital experiences, offerings and business models. Married to legacy business model—Burkett et al. (2017) prescribe unique leadership and talent to prevent a legacy culture from derailing a digital business initiative. Tiersky (2017) points out that real success in digital is rarely about providing the exact same products and services through a digital pipe.

> Netflix shifted from DVDs to streaming. Uber created the world's largest car service without buying any vehicles or hiring any drivers, and similarly eBay and Alibaba created the world's biggest retail channels without buying any inventory. Companies that successfully cross the chasm to digital effectiveness often discover they need to provide for free what they used to charge for, sell as a subscription what used to be a la carte, monetize via advertising things that used to be paid for in other ways, and re-think how they derive revenue from the value that they create. Those that do so flexibly can often find that the adoption of a digital strategy offers more scale, revenue and profit than the legacy approach, but it takes experimentation, an assumption of risk, and some failure along the way.
>
> Tiersky highlights that this approach is widely accepted among start-ups.

In summary, these challenges that occur through business transformation need to be addressed through expert project management, where expertise is built upon the lessons of previous projects.

References

Bloom, B. (2019), Should Your View of the Customer Be Singular or Plural? March 25.

Forbes. (2016), Why 84% of Companies Fail at Digital Transformation. Retrieved from https://www.forbes.com/sites/brucerogers/2016/01/07/why-84-of-companies-fail-at-digital-transformation/#5f1b943397bd.

Hammer, M., and Champy, J. (1993), *Reengineering the Corporation: A Manifesto for Business Revolution*. New York: Harper Collins.

Surowiecki, J. (2013), Where Nokia Went Wrong. *New Yorker*. Retrieved from https://www.newyorker.com/business/currency/where-nokia-went-wrong.

Taneja, H. (2019). Retrieved May 16, 2019, from https://hbr.org/2019/01/the-era-of-move-fast-and-break-things-is-over.

Tiersky, H. (2017), Navigating Digital Transformation. *CIO Magazine*. Retrieved from https://www.cio.com/article/3179607/e-commerce/5-top-challenges-to-digital-transformation-in-the-enterprise.html.

Gartner

Burkett et al. (2017), Make Digital Business Transformation a Practical Reality: A Gartner Trend Insight Report, ID: G00332548; Published: October 27, 2017 ID: G00332548; Analyst(s): Michael Burkett and Patrick Meehan.

Burton et al. (2016), Every Organisation Needs a Digital Platform Strategy, ID: G00316151, Gartner.

LeHong, Waller. (2017), Digital Business Ambition: Transform or Optimise? Gartner; Published: June 30, 2017 ID: G00333254; Analyst(s): Hung LeHong and Graham P. Waller.

Morello, D. (2016), Five Steps to Build Your Digital Business Dream Team; Published: March 21, 2016; Analyst(s): Diane Morello.

Prentice, B. (2017), Digital Business Transformation Strategy Needs a Change of Perspective, Gartner; Published: September 12, 2017 ID: G00332711; Analyst(s): Brian Prentice.

Swanton et al. (2017), A Digital Business Technology Platform Is Fundamental to Scaling Digital Business; Published: October 2, 2017 ID: G00342253; Analyst(s): Bill Swanton and Hung LeHong.

Waller. (2017), Master the Triple Tipping Point to Time Investments in Digital Business Strategy, Gartner; Foundational Refreshed: October 18, 2017; Published: February 9, 2016 ID: G00296107; Analyst(s): Graham P. Waller and Mark Raskino.

Waller, G., and Raskino, M. (2017), Master the Triple Tipping Point to Time Investments in Digital Business Strategy, Gartner; Foundational Refreshed: October 18, 2017; Published: February 9, 2016 ID: G00296107; Analyst(s): Graham P. Waller and Mark Raskino.

CHAPTER 2

Adapting Project Management to Meet This Challenge

Abstract Much evidence exists of companies going through business transformations but, there is little contemporary literature on how project management takes a role in this. The authors focus on why and how the business world view operations as the mainstay and not project management. The authors also examine the challenges faced by practitioners in the project management discipline and how it doesn't equip them well for transformational projects. It explores the gap between project management research and implementation. The discipline lacks a unified theory and established body of research that is widely accepted. Professional Bodies of Knowledge reflect process and technique and rely on practitioners interpreting this knowledge for transformation projects. The authors summarise the significance of learning from historical transformation projects to address the literature gaps.

Keyword Digital and business transformations

Introduction

The Project Management Institute (PMI) estimated in 2010 that 20% of the world's GDP, or more than $12 trillion annually, is spent on projects (Bredillet 2010). World Bank 2009 data estimated that 22% of the world's $48 trillion gross domestic product (GDP) was gross capital formation,

M. Kozak-Holland and C. Procter, *Managing Transformation Projects*, https://doi.org/10.1007/978-3-030-33035-4_2

which was almost entirely project-based. In India it is estimated to be 34%, and in China 45% [of GDP]. According to PMI (2017) 22 million new project-oriented jobs will be created between 2017 and 2027. This will include the majority of the world's most transformative projects, with an assumption that contemporary literature and methods can be adapted and customised by practitioners to achieve programme/project objectives.

The chapter examines the extent to which the role of project management in business transformation is analysed. It discusses how project management has evolved in both business and research literature and the relationship with operations management. It then argues for the importance for project management to learn from history and, specifically, the relevance of previous transformational projects to today's digital revolution.

The Role of Project Management in Transformation: The Industry View

Much evidence exists of companies going through transformation, yet there is little contemporary literature on how project management takes a role in this in.

Analyst journals like Gartner discuss digital transformation but with scant reference to the role of project management. Project management is seen as secondary to the transformation. Gartner discusses topics that are part of and even core to project management but outside of the context of project management. For example, there is substantial industry literature on agile and lean in the context of the transformation, discussed as if independent of project management. In fact, agile and lean approaches have in recent years become central and mainstream to project management (Beresford and Coelho 2018). By definition according to Pitagorsky (2006):

> Working lean means eliminating waste. Being agile is to be adaptive, resilient, flexible and appropriate to the situation.

Gartner recommends that organisations undertaking transformative projects borrow techniques and structures from project management such as a Program Office, aligning a set of projects to achieve business value, continuous iteration and delivery of software, without arguing for the strengthening of the project management role per se.

The Role of Project Management in Transformation: The Academic View

In academic journals there is very little literature at all concerning the role of project management in business transformation and the digital revolution, even in notable journals like the *Project Management Journal* (PMJ) or the *International Journal of Project Management* (IJPM). This is despite an understanding of the critical influence of project management on large project success (e.g. Flybjerg 2014).

Project management practitioner journals (*PMJ* and *IJPM*) literature on business transformation is also surprisingly sparse with just a few conference papers presented, for example at the PMI® Global Congress (Gopalakrishnan 2013).

Gopalakrishnan (2013) discusses the importance of practical project governance and:

> how a robust and stable governance model contributes to clarity of direction, cohesiveness of the team and alignment. An effective governance structure includes decision-making authority as well as an escalation path for issues that require attention from sponsors, leadership team, and quality and risk management teams. In addition, it provides a framework for transferring knowledge and building organisational capabilities to manage future complex projects.

Business journals, like the *Harvard Business Review*, provide some transformation case studies, but these are not project management specific, and contain scant details on the project. For example, with Adidas (2014):

> The whole project started from asking ourselves how to make a football better, adds Christian DiBenedetto, Adidas Senior Innovation Director.

Given the limited relevant research, the onus is on practitioners to improvise, customise and adapt project management frameworks to projects involving major change.

Project Management in the Business World

When universities set up the first business schools in the United States, in the early 1900s, operations management was emerging as an academic subject (Scranton 2010). Frederick Taylor and his work with Henry Ford, was central to this focus. The business school graduates introduced ideas to the business world and industry from the production line Ford Highland Park Detroit, and these best practices led to the birth of modern management. According to (Buffa 1984):

> As the study of business was growing, they [Taylor, Ford] were the practitioners-in-dominance. Taylor himself lectured at Harvard Business School and Henry Ford tirelessly promoted his approaches.

The leading players in industry were the US-based giants of the Second Industrial Revolution Ford, Standard Oil, General Electric, Bell and Goodyear. Shortly afterwards, management consulting was born as companies like Booz & Company (founded in 1914) copied Taylor's consultative approach based on his publication Principles of Scientific Management (1911). According to (Buffa 1984):

> The primacy of US and Fordist/Taylorist based approaches is an inheritance passed down to the current generation of operations academics, often without an appropriate level of questioning and consideration as to the dominant focus in Operations Management of recent US developments.

Contemporary management thinking is strongly rooted in this nineteenth-/twentieth-century legacy of management and operations.

The Roots of Contemporary Project Management

Morris (2013) describes how the history of contemporary project management is rooted in the post-Second World War zeal for science; just as international quality standards can trace their origins also to scientific methods of production in the war. This led to a discipline rooted in the scientific, hard, system-based mantra of the iron triangle (time, cost and scope) of project management. Morris et al. (2011, p. 16) suggest that:

> ...barring a few exceptions, it is not until the early 1950s that the language of contemporary project management begins to be invented.

Project management did not appear in the business mainstream as a discipline and management model until the 1960s coinciding with the spread of computers and IT (Garel 2012). Scranton argues that many organisations have struggled fitting projects and project management into their enterprise because of the operational paradigm (Scranton 2010). Other than high-profile corporate research and development divisions and product development units, other projects are viewed as peripheral or non-mainstream. Often projects are externalised through contracts, with high levels of specification. Organisations fit project management into an operational paradigm because operations are viewed as the raison d'etre of an organisation's existence.

Thus operations management can be in tension with project management with organisations trying to tame and contain the role of PM. This transforms projects into tasks without acknowledging the change they deliver, reformulating project ambiguities into 'known' elements and transforming their exploratory/reflexive functions into reporting and assessment (Boutinet 2004, pp. 82, 88–120).

What Is the Difference Between Operations and Project Management

To understand the fundamental differences requires a discussion on the definition of projects versus operations.

According to Lundin and Soderholm (1995), projects are temporary organisations with four dimensions: time limits and urgency, a focused target, a team orientation, and an emphasis on achieving change (transition). Scranton (2010) provides an explanation:

> First, time limits reference the start-up condition: the organisation is designed to vanish, whether successful or failing, whereas pressure for results is continuous, even intense.
>
> Second, the organisation has no warrant for self-definition; its targets have been framed by others, often by outsiders who have convened the enterprise as an instrument to achieve them.
>
> Third, because the means to the goal are not obvious or are complex, if understood, teamwork (not task assignment) is crucial, including feedback from multiple investigators, experiments, trials, designs-in use, et al., providing invaluable, critical reflexivity. Understanding who is on the team (individuals, firms, advisers), what their responsibilities are, how they were chosen and by whom is well worth knowing.
>
> Fourth, temporary organisations intended to reinforce the status quo are fakes; rather, a core challenge for them is to alter the present state of affairs, creating openings for workable, situated resolutions and perhaps longer-term transitions in orientation. Being alert to why these transitions/changes are

thought advisable or necessary leads us toward the four P"s namely, period, problem set, players, and performance.

Projects lean forward in time and reach into the unknown. They consider socio-cultural performance. They have unanticipated feedback loops. They are unstable, slippery and evolving, deal with uncertainty, and variable 'soft' people issues and not just 'hard' issues of resources and schedule.

Operations are the opposite in that they are permanent organisations that look back in time, steady state (no change), driven by operational routines and keep the lights on, and measure to improve (performance). They are stable, deal with the known, certain and hard, and invariable (non-changing).

The basic fundamental differences of Operations versus Projects are outlined in Fig. 2.1.

Operations

- **Permanent organization**
- **Look back in time**
- **Steady state**
- **Operational routines**
- **Keep the lights on**
- **Measure to improve**
- **Stable**
- **Are the known**
- **Certain**
- **Hard**
- **Invariable**

Project Management

- **Temporary organization**
- **Lean forward in time**
- **Project into the unknown**
- **Socio-cultural performance**
- **Unanticipated feedback loops**
- **Unstable, slippery & evolving**
- **Uncertain**
- **Soft**
- **Variable**

Fig. 2.1 The basic fundamental differences between the disciplines of Operations and Project Management

Operations are the mainstay of organisations, and according to Scranton (2010) some organisations simply operate and interact, and do not undertake projects:

> They make products, sell them directly to users or through intermediaries, or they provide services in an uncomplicated way. Most organisations perform projects. Projects are non-routine, going somewhere, with often either the route or the goal underdetermined, not-fully-formed or developed (inchoate), or ill defined (sometimes all three).

Scranton (2010) illustrates the difference by describing operations first:

> Enterprises, for-profit or not, act both inside their boundaries and across them, the former here termed operations and the latter interactions. The characteristics indicated under process, flows, outcomes, and rule set are suggested as typical, not uniform. In some operations, for example, authority may be hierarchical in general, but more collaborative within a specific unit, whereas some contracts may be entirely routinized.

Scranton (2010) then describes activities that only some enterprises attempt through projects:

> These efforts do not conform to the most common tasks within organisations or between them and clients, agencies, or competitors. Projects are non-routine, going somewhere, with often either the route or the goal underdetermined, inchoate, or ill defined (sometimes all three...).

These concepts are illustrated in Fig. 2.2. The terms that are at the core of project thinking are unknowable, reflexivity, improvisation and at the periphery of managerial (operations) thinking terms that express not an extension of operations (as do interactions between actors).

How Should Project Management Equip Project Managers for Business Transformation

Project management should be taking a leading role in business transformation. Project management bodies of knowledge do not however address this problem. Because project management has become operationalised, they do not necessarily equip project managers well for disruptive or transformational projects.

Core Activity	Operations	Interactions	Projects
Location	Inside org. boundary	Across org. boundary	Beyond org. boundary
Process	Routinized	Individualized	Exploratory
Flows	Hierarchical	Open-ended	Collaborative
Outcomes	Expected/predictable	Ritualized/dynamic	Unknowable
Rule set	Protocols/standards	Reciprocities	Reflexivity, improvisation
Examples	Accounting, reports, production, line mgt, evaluation	Contracts, sales, patents, licensing	One-off problem solving, innovation, experimental development

Fig. 2.2 A simplified sketch of organisational activity through interactions that occur either within, across (Operations) or outside (Projects) of organisational boundaries (Scranton 2010)

Traditional project management is not conducive to innovation, as the focus is on results and delivery. In many projects, innovation is often avoided because it can create uncertainty and increase costs. Project managers minimise risks by relying on tried and tested techniques, established routines and proven technologies. They select lowest cost approach, transfer risks to contractors, freeze the design as early as possible and stick rigidly to original plans (Davies et al. 2014). However, most large transformational projects are one-time opportunities; the opportunity to innovate may not exist after the project.

Traditional project management is not equipped to provide new emerging business models, but this is a critical characteristic in all business and digital transformation. It also may take years of trying before a new business model emerges; Netflix is an example.

Finally, it is questionable if established approaches meet the challenges of managing really large projects. Chapman (2016) argues:

> Against the backdrop of an emerging body of evidence, there are strong indications that traditional, linear project management tools and techniques, while essential, are insufficient to secure successful outcomes for today's most complex projects.

This is discussed further after the case studies in the conclusion.

Significance of Learning from the Examination of Historical Transformation Projects

As little project management literature was available until the mid-twentieth century a common perception among many project manager practitioners is that project management did not emerge as a discipline until then. Hence, the past has been overlooked because of the perception that project management is relatively new.

In fact, of course, megaprojects have existed for thousands of years as have transformational projects. For example, the Giza Pyramid was, for over 3500 years, the tallest building in the world, and is the only survivor of the original seven wonders of the world. It is thought to have been completed in less than 20 years in 2560 BCE without basic tools (such as the wheel) that would be taken for granted today. Giza was an infrastructure megaproject of its time. According to Flyvbjerg (2014):

> Megaprojects are large-scale, complex ventures that ... take many years to develop and build, involve multiple public and private stakeholders, are transformational, and impact millions of people.

The megaproject transformed ancient Egypt into a nation. The social, economic and political knowledge and resources of the world's first nation state were deployed to complete the project. Giza is one of many megaprojects from the past. According to Geraldi and Söderlund (2012):

> In arts and classic literature and in philosophy, people typically are aware of the wealth of knowledge found in the literature of the past. In management and organisation studies, this differs quite considerably. (Geraldi and Söderlund 2012, p. 561)

They go onto describe how the future of project management needs to learn from the past. They argue that project management research at present is too narrow and has too much focus on process and technique. According to Gaddis (2002):

> History isn't aimed at prediction, it is about understanding patterns and preparing ourselves to the future.

This in brief is the most significant point of learning from the examination of historical transformation projects; it better prepares practitioners understanding for the future.

Decontextualisation of Historical Case Studies

One important aspect that needs to be reviewed is the decontextualisation of historical case studies. For historians, comparing historical periods a few decades apart is problematic, because of the vast differences in context that change meaning. However, decontextualisation of management or project management lessons into sets of best practices is a common approach in today's business world and a starting point for almost all management consulting organisations. They have taken a pragmatic approach and have been down this path already in transferring best practices. They thrive on the commodification and creation of knowledge, between sectors and industries with a high degree of decontextualisation.

The Challenge for Project Managers

So how are these digital transformations delivered? Is it through projects? We don't have much empirical evidence. This illustrates the challenge faced by contemporary project managers in adopting best practice. There is a significant gap between project management research and implementation. The project management discipline lacks a unified theory and established body of research that is widely accepted. Professional Bodies of Knowledge reflect process and technique yet frequently neglect the political, social, ethical, economic and environmental dimensions of project management. They typically focus on the short-term results rather than long-term change. They do not thus necessarily equip managers well for disruptive or transformational projects, and the managers are well aware that their odds are not good.

Introduction to the Case-Studies

Case Study Selection

Based on the premise that project management has a deep history (Morris 2013), the following chapters examine three historical case studies in turn and demonstrate how the success of these projects can be demonstrated by the business transformation that they achieved. This is in contrast to the much narrower 'triple constraint' measurement of project success i.e., projects completed on time, to budget and to specification. In each chapter we examine the specific elements of the project management that contributed to transformation, which is summarised in the concluding Chapter 6.

The three historical projects are taken from previous industrial revolutions and are related to adapting emerging technologies to transport that had a major impact on transportation at the time. They were selected because they highlighted a very clear and substantial transformation that provided a significant economic gain and social impact. They all also involved the evolution of emerging technologies.

These case studies address the issues experienced in managing these projects. Historical project case studies are not constrained, and one clear advantage that they have over contemporary ones is that over time they are less likely to be subject to bias by the writer. They can also boldly go into areas that are highly sensitive and politically explosive to a contemporary organisation like executive (sponsor) decisions, or ethical behaviour. Flyvbjerg (2006, p. 242) contends:

> It is worth repeating the insight of Kuhn (1987): that a discipline without a large number of thoroughly executed case studies is a discipline without systematic production of exemplars, and that a discipline without exemplars is an ineffective one.

The case studies all also have a good historiography, which is well documented with supporting photographic evidence. They have been well analysed and written about from different domain perspectives (history, engineering, sociology).

The three projects examined are the Stockton and Darlington Railway and Manchester Ship Canal projects, both based in Great Britain, and the Trans Continental Railroad project in the United States. The core project management lessons are distilled from these case studies and summarised in the conclusion. Although each project initially set out to achieve business optimisation, all three resulted in significant business transformation and disruption. The lessons from these projects are very relevant to today's project managers.

Approach

Each chapter examines the case studies through a project management lens. They examine all the phases in a project: initiation, scope of the project and constraints, project procurement, project planning, project execution and project implementation. The chapters also analyse the decisions, sponsorship, leadership, organisational structure, culture and governance within the project providing a unique perspective on how the project unfolded.

References

Adidas miCoach Smart Ball Project. (2014). Retrieved February 16, 2019, from https://www.semiconductorstore.com/press/2014/adidas-miCoach-Smart-Ball/769.

Boutinet, J. (2004), *Anthropologie Du Projet* [Anthropology of the Project]. Paris: PUF.

Bredillet, C. (2010), Blowing Hot and Cold on Project Management. *Project Management Journal* 41 (3): 4–20.

Buffa, E. (1984). *Meeting the Competitive Challenge*. Irwin, IL.

Chapman, R. (2016), A Framework for Examining the Dimensions and Characteristics of Complexity Inherent Within Rail Megaprojects. *International Journal of Project Management* 34: 937–956.

Davies, A., MacAulay, S., DeBarro, T., and Thurston M. (2014), Making Innovation Happen in a Megaproject: London's Crossrail Suburban Railway System. *Project Management Journal* 45 (6): 25–37.

Flyvbjerg, B. (2006), Five Misunderstandings About Case-Study Research. *Qualitative Inquiry* 12 (2): 219–245.

Flyvbjerg, B. (2014), What You Should Know About Megaprojects and Why: An Overview. *Project Management Journal* 45 (2): 6–19.

Gaddis, J. (2002), *The Landscape of History: How Historians Map the Past*. New York: Oxford University Press.

Garel, G. (2012), A History of Project Management Models. *International Journal of Project Management* 21 (2013): 663–669.

Geraldi, J., and Söderlund, J. (2012), Classics in Project Management: Revisiting the Past, Creating the Future. *International Journal of Managing Projects in Business* 5 (4): 559–577.

Gopalakrishnan, B. (2013), Project Managing Global Business Transformation Projects: Tips and Tricks. Paper presented at PMI® Global Congress 2013—North America, New Orleans, LA. Newtown Square, PA: Project Management Institute.

Lundin, R., and Soderholm, A. (1995), A Theory of the Temporary Organisation. *Scandinavian Journal of Management* 11: 437–455 (quotes from 438).

Morris, P. (2013), Reconstructing Project Management (Wiley). Summarized latest book in an article for *Project Management Journal* 44 (5): 6–23.

Morris, P.W.G., Pinto, J.K., and Söderlund, J. (Eds.). (2011), *The Oxford Handbook of Project Management*. Oxford: Oxford University Press, pp. 15–36.

Pitagorsky, G. (2006), Agile and Lean Project Management: A Zen-Like Approach to Find Just the Right Degree of Formality for Your Project. Paper presented at PMI® Global Congress 2006—North America, Seattle, WA. Newtown Square, PA: Project Management Institute.

Scranton, P. (2010), *Projects as Business History: Surveying the Landscape*. New Brunswick, NJ: Rutgers University Press.

Gartner

Beresford, J., and Coelho, M. (2018), Scaling Enterprise Agility to Transform Established Organisations: BNP Paribas Fortis Bank, Gartner.

CHAPTER 3

Chapter Case Study 1: The Stockton and Darlington Railway

Abstract This project introduced an emerging technology into new usage in a sector, and then piloted and matured it to become operational. It proved its economic viability which led to an explosive growth of the British economy. The project addressed numerous unique obstacles including technical, legal and financial conflicts typical to contemporary transformation projects. The project owner was at the core of the success of the project as his leadership encouraged flexibility in the decision making and agility in the project that changed direction several times as explored alternatives were enacted, or unexpected opportunities were exploited. He also enabled innovation in the project, by setting up a factory which allowed the extensive prototyping and piloting of new technologies, reduction of risks and successful implementation.

Keywords Project sponsor role · Incorporating agility · Entrepreneurial partnerships · Exploiting unexpected opportunities · Technology innovation · Prototyping and piloting · Knowledge capture

Introduction

The Stockton and Darlington Railway (SDR) project started life as the most cost efficient way of moving coal from mine to coast for shipping: it was essentially a project to optimise existing process. Rail was selected as

M. Kozak-Holland and C. Procter, *Managing Transformation Projects*, https://doi.org/10.1007/978-3-030-33035-4_3

being more optimal than horse and cart. The technical innovations involved in the project and the entirely novel idea of transporting passengers as well as freight led to it becoming arguably one of the most significant transformation projects of the nineteenth century. The construction of the world's first commercial railway was significant to proving the viability of the technology and enabling massive growth of the British economy. The completion of the project involved addressing numerous unique obstacles including technical, legal and financial conflicts. Despite these, the project met its specifications, was completed effectively and was profitable after a longer than expected payback period.

At the heart of the success of the project was the commitment from the project owner, Edward Pease and his consortium of Quaker investors, and their commercial partnership. This entrepreneurial partnership and leadership enabled innovation in the project and led to the setting up of a factory in conjunction with the Chief Engineer George Stephenson which allowed the piloting of new technologies, reduction of risks and successful implementation.

Background

Early forms of railway evolved in the mining industry. By the fifteenth century wagons were pushed on wooden wagon-ways. Gradually horse-drawn wagons were developed and introduced in Germany in the 1550s (Agricola 1913) and then spread across Europe in late sixteenth and seventeenth centuries. Advances in technology (cast and wrought iron) first led to protective iron strips nailed to protect the rails (Clark 1985) and then replaced the horse-drawn wagons with a horse-drawn tramway with iron rails and wheels. By the middle of the eighteenth century stationary steam engines were generally available in mining and used for wagon-ways with steep uphill sections.

Project Initiation

Edward Pease, a north east wool merchant, initiated the project to solve the problem of transporting large volumes of coal from Darlington to Stockton-on-Tees with its port and access to the North Sea. His woollen mills and other interests would benefit from this. Darlington, in County Durham, was one of the richest mineral fields in the north of England with vast reserves of coal. Coal from the inland mines had been traditionally carried on packhorses, and then as the roads were improved, on horse and carts. Poor roads to market made coal transport by horse and cart very expensive, and almost closed the mines.

Scope of the Project and Constraints

Pease needed to find funding for a perceived risky project. As a very well-connected Quaker business entrepreneur, he created a consortium to finance a project to build a canal from Stockton on the coast to Darlington to exploit a rich vein of coal. The route ran into some public opposition (Allen 1974, p. 16). A canal had been proposed by George Dixon in 1767 and again by John Rennie in 1815, but both schemes failed to gain enough support to get the required parliamentary permissions.

A number of key decisions were made affecting the direction of the project.

Project Decision #1 Related to the Type of Transportation System

A few years later Pease considered proposing a canal on a route that bypassed Darlington and Yarm, and a meeting was held locally in Yarm to oppose the route. He presented a private bill to Parliament. However, this bill was changed after Pease consulted with a Welsh engineer George Overton, who advised building a tram road instead. This was a key decision; either to go with a tried and tested system (canals/barges) that was very well established or innovate something new (rails or tramway). A horse-drawn barge could pull 40 tons along a canal, whereas a horse-drawn tramway could pull 10 tons. A tramway opened up future opportunities. Pease went with the recommendation and the rationale that it was an opportunity to innovate.

Overton carried out a survey and planned a route (Tomlinson 1915, pp. 45–47). The original survey recommended a canal priced at £95,600. The new survey favoured a railway (horse drawn) scheme at £124,000.

Project Decision #2 Related to the Type of Rail Transportation System

The second major decision related to whether to go with a horse-drawn tramway or create something new, like a stationary steam engine. Although a horse-drawn tramway could pull 10 tons, a steam drawn tramway with stationary engines could dramatically increase speed, load and decrease cost. This could provide an opportunity to open up future business opportunities.

The initial decision was to go with a horse-drawn tramway with two cable-worked inclines at the western end operated by stationary steam engines. George Stephenson became aware of the project and sought out Pease to see if he could interest him in a vision and alternative transportation ideas he had. He was a self-taught engineer with the desire to increase his steam railway experience. He wanted to share some of the larger practical field knowledge he had already gained.

He impressed Pease by advocating the potential of using moveable engines or steam locomotives on a tram road or railway line. Stephenson told Pease that a horse on an iron road would draw ten tons for one ton on a common road. Stephenson added that the Blucher locomotive that he had built at Killingworth colliery was worth fifty horses (Ashton 1948).

Pease visited Killingworth (Tomlinson 1915, p. 439) and when he saw the Blucher at work he realised that George Stephenson was right and offered him the post of Chief Engineer in the project responsible for its execution and a position in the Stockton and Darlington Company with an annual salary of £300.

Pease advocated this at a public meeting in Darlington on 13 November 1818, promising a 5% return on investment (Tomlinson 1915, pp. 45–47; Allen 1974, pp. 16–17). Approximately 66% of the shares were sold locally, and the rest were bought by Quakers nationally. Pease was interested even then in the possibility of creating a rail network across the UK.

A private bill was presented to Parliament in March 1819, but as the route passed through the Earl of Eldon's estate and one of the Earl of Darlington's fox coverts, it was opposed and defeated by 13 votes. The route was changed with agreement for the line not to pass through the estate and a bill was lodged on 30 September 1820. Pease subscribed £7000 and from that time he had considerable influence over the railway which became known as the Quaker line.

The recommendations made by Stephenson resulted in adding a clause to the Act that stated that Parliament gave permission for the company to make and erect locomotives or moveable engines, and the Act was passed on 19 April 1821. It allowed for a railway to be used by anyone with suitably built vehicles on payment of a toll that would be closed at night, and with which land owners within 5 miles (8 km) could build branches and make junctions (Tomlinson 1915, p. 70; Kirby 2002, p. 37).

Project Planning

On 23 July 1821 it was decided that the line would be a railway with edge rails, rather than a plateway (flat rails), and Stephenson was appointed to make a fresh survey of the line (Tomlinson 1915, p. 74). The line included embankments up to 48 feet (15 m) high. By the end of 1821 he had reported that a usable line could be built within the bounds of the Act, but another route would be shorter by 3 miles (5 km) and avoid deep cuttings and tunnels (Allen 1974, p. 20).

Project Execution

At this point several solutions were identified; namely, horse-drawn tramways, stationary engines pulling wagons, and steam locomotives, all to run along an 8 miles (12.9 km) railway, line. In 1822 Stephenson recommended trialing locomotives based on past experience with stationary steam engines. The options were to add steam locomotives to stationary engines or stay with stationary engines. There were a number of advantages for a steam locomotive over a stationary engine; namely greater traction on rails and more horsepower for pulling. The technology was more flexible over different terrains and provided better possibilities to grow a rail network. It would be easier to assemble and manufacture, easier to fix or maintain and more reliable.

The decision was made to add steam locomotives to stationary engines on a shorter route to avoid cuttings and tunnels. The rationale was that stationary engines were somewhat limited, and locomotives would speed up the operation. Although locomotives were very expensive, unproven and risky, they had proven to be effective at Killingworth colliery (Allen 1974, pp. 76–78). The principal challenge was that the SDR was 9 times the length, and thus a far greater distance for moving locomotives and building rail tracks, with substantial complications in the terrain requiring bridges.

According to Smiles (1857) steam technology was still in its infancy so George Stephenson and his son Robert Stephenson formed a company in 1823 to make locomotives, the Robert Stephenson & Company, the world's first locomotive builder. They invested and set up a locomotive factory at Forth Street, Newcastle upon Tyne, where they went through various proofs-of-concepts and pilots. Stephenson recruited Timothy Hackworth, one of the engineers who had helped William Hedley to produce

Puffing Billy, an earlier locomotive built in 1813, to work for the company. They employed skilled mechanics. This was a large investment and risk for them, but the immature technology was essential to the project. They determined the best combination of small to large wheels to aid propulsion, rail type (wrought-iron versus cast-iron or a mix), gauge, etc. They source technologies for defined needs/gaps like the long (wrought) iron rails pioneered by John Birkinshaw. He then partnered with William Losh manufacturing company to build the cast-iron rails (Figs. 3.1, 3.2, and 3.3).

The factory goal was to improve the performance in steam engine components with:

Fig. 3.1 Stephenson's locomotive manufactory at Newcastle upon Tyne as it evolved, the lathe and tool shop. The factory was critical to the project piloting of emerging technologies (The *Illustrated London News*, 1864, John Weedy's Collection of *Illustrated London News*)

Fig. 3.2 Stephenson's locomotive manufactory at Newcastle upon Tyne as it evolved, the fitting-shop. The factory provided a space to experiment with emerging technologies (The *Illustrated London News*, 1864, John Weedy's Collection of *Illustrated London News*)

- More efficient transfer of motion
- Higher temperature and steam pressures
- Reduced vibration making the engine more stable

In their factory they established manufacturing processes and from this developed improvements like inclined cylinders to prevent excess rocking, and a multi-tube boiler and a separate firebox. From this the first locomotive standards started to emerge.

The project procured four stationary engines (2 × 30 hp, 2 × 15 hp) for two inclines and 2 travelling locomotives at £500 each (Fig. 3.4).

Fig. 3.3 Stephenson's locomotive manufactory at Newcastle upon Tyne as it evolved, the steam-hammer (The *Illustrated London News*, 1864, John Weedy's Collection of *Illustrated London News*)

Project Decision #3 Related to the Type of Rail Track System and Rail Gauge

The third decision related to the type of material, its shape and gauge. Rail tracks were in their infancy with no standards set. Rail tracks (over plates) with wheels provided:

- Less friction, with better traction on track
- Fewer issues over greater distances
- Extended lifespan

The options available were cast-iron rails which were still in their infancy and excessively brittle versus wrought iron rails, a new technology that made rail more malleable, with less cracking or bending, and carries a greater weight. Pease and Stephenson decided on a mix of wrought-iron rails 66% and cast-iron 33%. The rails were produced in longer lengths and as a result were less likely to crack. The rationale was they required fewer joints and

Fig. 3.4 Locomotion No. 1 opened the Stockton and Darlington Railway in 1825 (*The Engineer*, 1875, Grace's Guide Collection)

were a financially better option. The rails were set 4 feet 8½ inches (1.42 m) apart (Kirby 2002, pp. 61–63), the same gauge used by Stephenson on his Killingworth Railway. The 4 feet 8½ gauge was the same gauge for carts and wagons and was later adopted as a standard over much of the world.

Work on the 26 miles track began in 1822 with a ceremony in Stockton that celebrated the laying of the first track at St John's Well 23 May 1822. Stephenson used malleable iron rails carried on cast iron chairs. These rails were laid on wooden blocks for 12 miles between Stockton and Darlington. The 15 miles track from the collieries near Shildon, and Darlington were laid on stone blocks.

Most of the track used 28 lb/yd (14 kg/m) of malleable iron rails. 4 miles (6.4 km) of 57.5 lb/yd (28.5 kg/m) cast-iron rails were used for junctions (Tomlinson 1915, pp. 89–90). By 1823, 22 of 26 miles of rail were laid.

The project team identified and created next-generation technology in locomotives and rails through the partnerships they had established early in the project.

Stephenson's project approach was to:

1. Increase his fundamental knowledge in core technologies through prototypes made in his factory.

2. Source technologies for defined needs/gaps like the long (wrought) iron rails pioneered by John Birkinshaw.
3. Identify the development trends relevant to railways, and how a core business (moving goods but expanding to passengers) could be developed around this, aware of competitors (e.g., horse-drawn transport).
4. Identify next-generation technology, in locomotives and rails, in their early stages.
5. Connect with the technical community in locomotives and rails (partnership with William Losh in manufacturing cast-iron rails).

Project Decision #4 Related to the Type of Bridges in Material and Construction

The project identified 2 essential river crossings. The two rivers required the first railway bridge in the world to carry the weight of a fully laden train (100 tons). The bridges had to be reliable, cost effective, simple construction, carry a large moving load and have an extended lifetime. Options were stone, iron (cast or wrought) or timber. Iron bridge technology was still in its infancy. The decision was to go with both the stone and iron type. The rationale was the first iron bridge at Coalbrookdale had demonstrated how the new technology could be applied. Stephenson designed a wrought-iron girder bridge to cross the River Gaunless. It combined both arch and suspension principles of construction, both cast and wrought iron with different properties, compression versus tension and bending.

The Iron Railway Bridge was truly innovative as it was lighter and cheaper than stone, easier to assemble and construct, more reliable and able to carry the full load of a 100 ton moving train (Fig. 3.5).

The River Skerne has a wider span, so the committee decided on a stone bridge and which was designed by the Durham architect Ignatius Bonomi (Hoole 1974, pp. 173–174).

Project Decision #5 Related to Goods Versus Passenger Transportation

Rail for passengers was in its infancy. The parliamentary bill included provisions for passengers although this was regarded as just a sideline. The decision was to include both in the bill since there could be a case in the

Fig. 3.5 First iron railway bridge was over the River Gaunless on the Stockton and Darlington Railway, and was designed by Robert Stephenson (*The Engineer*, 1875, Grace's Guide Collection)

future for passenger transportation. In 1807 the first fare-paying, horse-drawn passenger railway service had been established on the Oystermouth Railway in Swansea, Wales. The line was single track with four passing loops each mile (Allen 1974, p. 27); square sleepers supported each rail separately so that horses could walk between them (Rolt 1984, p. 75).

Project Procurement

In 1824 the SDR ordered two steam locomotives and two stationary engines from the Robert Stephenson and Company (Hoole 1974, p. 188). Advertising proclaimed that the railway would open on 27 September 1825 (Tomlinson 1915, p. 105).

Project Implementation

Stephenson and Pease literally stumbled into the concept of passenger rail when, as a publicity stunt, they offered on their grand opening day, 27 September 1825, for people to ride in the freight wagons for a penny. Existing passenger land transportation depended on coaches drawn by horses. Over 40,000 people showed up to travel faster than a horse, a whole new experience for future customers. According to Tomlinson (1915, pp. 110–112):

> The directors had allowed room for 300 passengers, but the train left carrying between 450 and 600 people, most travelling in empty waggons but some on top of waggons full of coal. Brakesmen were placed between the waggons, and the train set off, led by a man on horseback with a flag. It picked up speed on the gentle downward slope and reached 10 to 12 miles per hour (16 to 19 km/h), leaving behind men on field hunters (horses) who had tried to keep up with the procession. The train stopped when the waggon carrying the company surveyors and engineers lost a wheel; the waggon was left behind, and the train continued. The train stopped again, this time for 35 minutes to repair the locomotive and the train set off again, reaching 15 mph (24 km/h) before it was welcomed by an estimated 10,000 people as it came to a stop at the Darlington branch junction. Eight and a half miles (14 km) had been covered in two hours and subtracting the 55 minutes accounted by the two stops, it had travelled at an average speed of 8 mph (13 km/h). Six waggons of coal were distributed to the poor, workers stopped for refreshments and many of the passengers from Brusselton alighted at Darlington, to be replaced by others.

Pease and Stevenson had the makings of a new business model which could help boost revenues to support the fledgling model of freight transport. The SDR became the world's first commercial railway with far reaching disruptive consequences.

Emerging Operational Model

Initially, a mix of transportation types was allowed to run on the line simultaneously, stationary steam engines, travelling locomotives and horses that could haul up to four wagons. But this caused chaos because of the different speeds. From this the owners established processes for an operational model that quickly moved away from the canal paradigm, free-for-all any type of barge, to eliminating horse-drawn transport and moving entirely to locomotives. They also fought off a hostile takeover by a horse-drawn transport consortium.

Project Outcome

The train also included a purpose-built railway passenger coach called the Experiment. The carriage seated 18 passengers, and as it had no springs it must have provided an uncomfortable ride but for the first time in history, a steam locomotive had hauled passengers on a public railway.

The cost of building the railway had greatly exceeded the estimates. By September 1825 the company had borrowed £60,000 in short-term loans and needed to start earning an income to ward off its creditors. The project had greatly exceeded the initial cost estimates by 50% and was in very deep financial trouble. Debt prevented any expansion work. According to Tomlinson (1915, pp. 138–140):

> The railway opened with the company owing money and unable to raise further loans; Pease advanced money twice early in 1826 so the workers could be paid. By August 1827 the company had paid its debts and was able to raise more money; that month the Black Boy branch opened, and construction began on the Croft and Hagger Leases branches. During the course of 1827 shares rose in value from £120 at the start to £160.

The railway carried goods and made an immediate return:

> Initially the line was used to carry coal to Darlington and Stockton, carrying 10,000 tons in the first three months and earning nearly £2,000. In Stockton the price of coal dropped from 18 to 12 shillings, and by the beginning of 1827 was 8 shillings 6 pence (8s 6d) (Tomlinson 1915, pp. 117, 119). Initially the drivers had been paid a daily wage, but after February 1826 they were paid 1/penny per ton per mile; from this they had to pay assistants and fireman and to buy coal for the locomotive (Tomlinson 1915, p. 132). The 1821 Act had received opposition from the owners of collieries on the River Wear who supplied London and feared competition. Thus, the rate for transporting coal destined for ships was restricted to 1 penny per ton per mile, which had been assumed would make the business uneconomic.

There was sufficient demand from London for 100,000 tons a year, so the company began investigations in September 1825:

> In January 1826 the first staith[1] opened at Stockton, designed so waggons over a ship's hold could discharge coal from the bottom (Tomlinson 1915, pp. 120–121). A little over 18,500 tons of coal was transported to ships in the year ending June 1827 and this increased to over 52,000 tons the following year (53). (Tomlinson 1915, p. 136)

Expansion was limited to only revenue generating opportunities and planned branch lines to Coundon or Croft were not built for this reason.

Impact on Economy

This new railway initiated the construction of more railway lines, causing significant developments in railway mapping and cartography, iron and steel manufacturing, as well as in any industries requiring more efficient transportation (Challis and Rush 2009).

Conclusion

The most innovative aspect of the project was to prove the commercial viability of railways. Steam transport was more expensive than horse drawn, but the project proved it to be viable and economic after a period in operation.

The key innovations were how the project integrated all components of a railway system and demonstrated the commercial feasibility of developing a line of usable length. The Stephenson's factory was central to this success and was used to build the more sophisticated Rocket locomotive for the Manchester-Liverpool Railway in 1830.

Every nation copied the British model. A railway revolution commenced in the UK in 1830, and then swept across Europe and North America around 1840 and had a profound impact on all the respective economies. For example, in the UK at its peak (1845–1847) railways accounted for 50% of all UK domestic capital formation (Barras 2009). Railways enabled gradual development of a national market: goods were produced on a mass scale in a decreasing number of centres and were then distributed by rail around the country.

[1] A staith is an elevated platform used to transfer minerals such as coal from railway waggons onto ships staith. Webster's Unabridged Dictionary. Project Gutenberg. Retrieved 8 March 2014.

The SDR project lasted 3 years and was completed in 1825 at a cost of £5.1m (in today's money). The railways were the future as accurately predicted by Stephenson:

> George Stephenson told me as a young man that railways will supersede almost all other methods of conveyance in this country… [they] will become the great highway for the king and all his subjects.

Engineer John Dixon-quoted by Samuel Smiles in his Life of George Stephenson (Smiles 1857). Stephenson was the guiding spirit of the railway age.

Project Management Lessons

The chapter now analyses the case study and explores a wide range of project management lessons arising from it to draw out lessons of contemporary value.

The Role of the Project Sponsor

In this case study Pease's role was critical in providing a vision (with Stephenson), understanding the political landscape and constraints, and being flexible to new ideas. His industry experience as a businessman and entrepreneur willing and able to take a loss on his investment was essential to putting together a consortium to fund and drive the project. When Stephenson approached him, he was willing to change direction on the approach and technology, quickly recognising the opportunity. Pease stepped in at critical points in the project where it potentially could get into trouble and took actions to mitigate the risk.

The role and responsibilities of the project sponsor need to be clearly understood by all the project stakeholders from initiating the project, to rallying support, shaping project objectives and direction. This is especially important when it comes to removing numerous obstacles including technical, legal, financial and political issues. In disruptive projects the sponsor may be asked to play an active part in the management of the project.

Creating Entrepreneurial Partnerships

In the SDR project Pease encouraged Stephenson to open up a factory where entrepreneurial partnerships were established to enable innovation. Pease nurtured leadership to drive innovation for the benefit of the project.

This substantially lowered the project risk and ensured a smoother operation. Stephenson and his son Robert, along with three partners, opened the world's first purpose built locomotive works. He saw this factory as part of the long-term vision and is proved correct as it successfully produced next generation technology locomotives for this and future projects (i.e., the Rocket for the Manchester-Liverpool Railway in 1830). The factory subsequently exported locomotives to developing railways all over the world. In contemporary project management and transformation the creation of entrepreneurial partnerships is important in setting up all the required elements of a project and insourcing the required knowledge and skills to cover existing gaps and to help create a solution. This relates to all aspects from project financing, to contracts, to emerging technologies. According to Carlsson (2004):

> The role of entrepreneurs is to identify profitable innovations among all the technical possibilities and convert them into business opportunities. In order to do so, entrepreneurs need support in the form of venture capital (not just risk capital but also the business competence required to develop suitable strategies as well as identify and acquire key resources, including personnel).

Exploiting Unexpected Opportunities

Pease and Stephenson assessed and exploited unexpected opportunities that were discovered in the project. Switching from a canal to a horse-drawn tramway and then to locomotion required innovation to open up future opportunities. This necessitated significant and risky decisions requiring a major change in technology. For example, the steam engine was too heavy for roads or wooden track and required iron rails that were still in their infancy requiring substantial new development. The project procurement of stationary engines and locomotives highlights the need to be open to opportunities through the project, and then seizing the most lucrative of these, and making significant investments to maximise the opportunity. The risks were high initially, but the experimental space provided an environment to run proofs-of-concepts and pilots and evolve technologies and processes.

In contemporary transformative projects the project team needs to be ready for unexpected opportunities and to have the necessary processes in place to evaluate and then exploit them. This requires clear understanding of the business case and its basis, so as to be able to assess new unexpected opportunities and put them into perspective. Very often these can have a greater payback than the original business case, so a decision needs to be made as to whether they are incorporated into the project or merit their own project. This is the essence of agile.

Technology Innovation
The technology was under-developed, untried and untested. The locomotive factory provided a conducive environment to understand and evolve it. The Blucher locomotive at Killingworth could haul 8 wagons or 30 tons of coal at 4 mph over a distance of 3 miles. The goal was to double or triple the speed, in fact, locomotion could reach up to 15 mph. All parts of this transportation system had to undergo innovation and improvements, from the rail tracks to the propulsion and traction. In contemporary project management and transformation, using technology innovation, in both products and processes, to create solutions is critical. It can reduce the project scope and cost in activities on the critical path. For example, once a product is developed the technology innovation is relatively small. Often competitors don't focus on evolving the product, but the actual processes around the product in how it is used, and this is evolved and improved.

Extensive Prototyping and Piloting
The SDR project required extensive prototyping and piloting to evolve and adapt various new emerging technologies for transportation solutions. For example, creating a steam engine powerful enough to reach the target speeds required substantial improvements in the performance of steam engine components or the combustion chambers.

Today, extensive prototyping and piloting is pivotal when working with solutions that are based on emerging technologies. Otherwise there are substantial risks that this helps to mitigate. Piloting is tolerant of stumbles and failures, and a safe space for reflexivity. This critical project step also determines and estimates how the pilot is scaled-up to create a production ready solution.

Incorporating Agility into Projects so as to Change Course in Response to Emerging Opportunities and Threats
The project took a number of substantial changes in direction as transportation alternatives were evaluated for their pay-back (project and long-term), feasibility, ability to complete and risk. This flexibility required a relatively high level of agility to accommodate a high degree of uncertainty.

Being nimble and quick can be crucial to the overall success for several reasons. Rapid changes in technology over short periods have to be accommodated in a project. Technology enables new applications and capabilities that open new business opportunities.

An agile project recognises and welcomes the change that technology will have on the project. Technology roadmaps are identified, using techniques like technology landscape mapping which plot the maturity of a technology in its evolution over the course of time. Recognition of the inevitability of change was fundamental to the evolution of Agile in the late twentieth century: Responding to change over following a plan was a key component of the original Agile manifesto. While Agile originated in software development and is of great significance to contemporary IT projects (e.g., Jørgensen 2018; Dingsoyr et al. 2012), it is great relevance to all project management (e.g., Serrador and Pinto 2015; Lensges et al. 2018). Agility of course can increase risk and thus learning from the effective adoption of an agile approach from a historical project can provide important lessons for contemporary projects.

Mandating Knowledge Capture

The project team, under Stephenson, had to increase their fundamental knowledge in core technologies. For Stephenson this was critical for the project and the future of railways. Stephenson recruited Timothy Hackworth, one of the engineers from the Puffing Billy project and national expert. He also employed skilled mechanics who could quickly put ideas into practical use and innovate the manufacturing processes for the locomotive.

In contemporary project management and transformation, mandating knowledge capture and transfer between projects is essential, so future projects are part of a continuum, especially where the technology is similar and evolving quickly. This becomes a challenge where multiple projects start up simultaneously. The Project Management Office has an important role to play in establishing in the organisation smooth knowledge transfer, and also in forming enterprise views of architectures (business, solution, technical). This is akin to planning the infrastructure within a city environment.

Summary

The SDR had a transformational impact on passenger transport. The first passenger railway in the United States opened just three years after the opening of the SDR (1828—see Chapter 4) and the famous Liverpool and Manchester railway in the UK opened in 1830.

The SDR project provides important lessons in the challenges involved in introducing an emerging technology into new usage in a sector, and then maturing so it can become operational and economically viable. The prize was the transformation of transportation that had a major economic impact. The project was mired in unique obstacles including legal conflicts, technical and financial difficulties. But strong leadership from the business (Pease) and technical (Stephenson) sides of the project ensured that these obstacles were removed. Pease leveraged his consortium of Quaker investors. Stephenson organised his factory to pilot the technologies and reduce the risks. Even then the outcome was unknown until the realisation that the commercial passenger market could be made viable, not fully envisioned in the first place or within the business case. The project that had started with the scope of optimising the movement of coal, ended by disrupting passenger transportation in the UK and thence the world.

References

Agricola, G. (1913), *De re Metallica*, trans. Hoover. New York: Dover, p. 156.

Allen, Cecil J. (1974 [1964]), *The North Eastern Railway*. Shepperton: Ian Allan.

Ashton, T. (1948), *The Industrial Revolution 1760–1830*. Oxford: Oxford University Press, p. 71.

Barras, R. (2009), *Building Cycles: Growth and Instability*. Chichester: Wiley.

Carlsson, B. (2004), The Digital Economy: What Is New and What Is Not? *Structural Change and Economic Dynamics* 15: 245–264.

Challis, David Milbank, and Rush, Andy. (2009), The Railways of Britain: An Unstudied Map Corpus. *Imago Mundi* 61 (2): 186–214. https://doi.org/10.1080/03085690902923614.

Clark, R. (1985), *Works of Man: History of Invention and Engineering, from the Pyramids to the Space Shuttle* (1st American Edition, 8 × 10 Hard cover ed.). New York: Viking Penguin, p. 352 (indexed).

Dingsoyr, T., Nerur, S., Balijepally, V., and Moe, N. B. (2012), A Decade of Agile Methodologies: Towards Explaining Agile Software Development. *Journal of Systems and Software*, 85: 1213–1221. https://doi.org/10.1016/j.jss.2012.02.033

Hoole, K. (1974), *A Regional History of the Railways of Great Britain: Volume IV the North East.* Exeter: David & Charles.

Jørgensen, M. (2018), Do Agile Methods Work for Large Software Projects? https://doi.org/10.1007/978-3-319-91602-6_12, *Agile Processes in Software Engineering and Extreme Programming*, 19th International Conference, XP 2018, Porto, Portugal, May 21–25, 2018, Proceedings.

Kirby, M. (2002), *The Origins of Railway Enterprise: The Stockton and Darlington Railway 1821–1863.* Cambridge: Cambridge University Press.

Lensges, M., Kloppenborg, T. J., and Forte, F. (2018), Identifying key Agile Behaviors that Enhance Traditional Project Management Methodology. *Journal of Strategic Innovation and Sustainability*, 13 (2): 22–36.

Rolt, L.T.C. (1984), *George and Robert Stephenson: The Railway Revolution.* London: Penguin.

Serrador, P., and Pinto, J. (2015), Does Agile work?—A Quantitative Analysis of Agile Project Success. *International Journal of Project Management*, 33. https://doi.org/10.1016/j.ijproman.2015.01.006.

Smiles, S. (1857), *The Life of George Stephenson and of His Son Robert Stephenson: Comprising Also a History of the Invention and Introduction of the Railway Locomotive.* New York: Harper Brothers.

Tomlinson, William Weaver. (1915), *The North Eastern Railway: Its Rise and Development.* Newcastle upon Tyne: Andrew Reid & Co.

CHAPTER 4

Chapter Case Study 2: The Transcontintental Railroad

Abstract This was the world's most significant infrastructure projects of the nineteenth century. The leadership in the US government set up entrepreneurial commercial partnership which enabled the innovation in the project and this allowed it to conquer substantial risks and succeed. The private sector could not take on a project of this magnitude with the level of risk involved so the project owner was critical in fostering commercial relationships and partnerships, supported by financing, through government acts. Project reflexivity and course correction were critical. The project was completed 7 years ahead of schedule; incredible for such an ambitious project. The construction of a railroad that spanned the United States contributed significantly to the growth of the economy, and development of the United States as a global economic power.

Keywords Project sponsor role · Defining business case · Governance · Risk and window of opportunity · Driving innovation in megaprojects · Creating high morale culture · Uncertainty and complexity · Prototyping and piloting · Project reflexivity · Transition to operations

M. Kozak-Holland and C. Procter, *Managing Transformation Projects*, https://doi.org/10.1007/978-3-030-33035-4_4

Introduction

The Transcontinental Railroad (TCR) was arguably one of the world's most significant infrastructure projects of the nineteenth century. The construction of a railroad that spanned the United States contributed significantly to the growth of the economy, and development of the United States as a global economic power. The completion of the project involved addressing numerous unique obstacles including technical, legal, financial and military conflicts. Despite these, the project met its specifications, was completed early, and its cost in government debt was paid off in full.

At the heart of the success of the project was the commitment from the project owner and sponsor, US President Abraham Lincoln, and the US government, and their commercial partnership with two companies, Union Pacific Railroad (UPRR) and Central Pacific Railroad (CPRR) who developed the railroad from east and west respectively. It was a partnership born from the necessities of the US Civil War, 1861–1865, as a result of the long-standing controversy over the enslavement of black people (Hutchison 2015). This entrepreneurial partnership and leadership enabled the innovation in the project which allowed it to conquer substantial risks and succeed.

This case study is set in the context of a substantial and growing body of knowledge examining the success and failure of megaprojects, and specifically infrastructure megaprojects, and in contemporary research into effective project partnerships and innovation. The lessons of success from the TCR project are of considerable relevance to today's infrastructure megaprojects.

The TCR project was thought of as practically impossible because of the immense geographical challenges it faced. The proposed project route ran from the Missouri river to the Pacific Ocean over 2000 miles with little or no existing wagon tracks. In the West the route would encounter peaks of over 7000 feet, massive ravines, dense forests and deserts. Aside from these geographic challenges the project also faced enormous technical challenges. Nothing on this scale of railroad development had ever been attempted: the project idea was advanced only some 30 years after the world's first commercial railway line (i.e., the SDR) was built over a length of 26 miles! There were also substantial legal issues (contracts, land grants, workers' and settlers' rights), financial (investments) and the project was initiated during the American civil war. The project required the ability to pull together the right expertise that could then be fostered to innovate and evolve solutions to these challenges.

Innovation can occur in projects but unsurprisingly it is not encouraged because it can create uncertainty and increase costs. Project managers minimise risk by relying on tried-and-tested techniques, established routines and proven technologies. They select the lowest cost approach, transfer risks to contractors, freeze the design early, and stick rigidly to the plan (Davies et al. 2014). This case study explores this problem of introducing and fostering innovation in a megaproject.

The textual evidence concerning the construction of the TCR is reliable as the megaproject had significant exposure in the media. Today there are many first-hand accounts of people involved and newspapers that covered the project.

Background—The History of US Railroad Building

US railroad building had copied British technology and practices (short runs between towns) and had begun with the Baltimore-Ohio Railroad in 1828 which started a railroad mania. The concept of a TCR was first discussed in public when the Pacific Railroad Surveys were completed (1853–1855) extensively mapping the American West. The surveys calculated the scope of the various routes (2000 miles) and the degree of difficulty in constructing them. US railroad building lacked a history of railroad project experience on the scale of the TCR. The British Government had built the Grand Trunk Railroad (1852) in Canada at over 500 miles long but it turned into a financial disaster (Carlos and Lewis 1995), as they had failed to adapt practices from the UK to deal with conditions in Canada, namely distance and climate. By 1860 the railroad verged on bankruptcy and was bailed out by the British government in Canada. But by 1861, lines ran 1118 miles (1800 kms) Sarnia to Quebec City and Portland, Maine.

Project Initiation

Project Decision #1 1862 Pacific Railroad Acts Passed to Initiate Project

Lincoln realised that to build a transcontinental railroad required major innovation initiated through government acts and contracts, and then fostered through the project. The project was initiated in 1862 with the Pacific Railroad Act (The Pacific Railroad Act, n.d.) US Senate where lawmakers resolved to do enough, and only enough, to induce capitalists to build the

Pacific railway (Launius 1965). The timing seems very irrational and at odds with the Civil War raging but, Lincoln understood how the war had changed politics, so it was a one-time opportunity to get the Act(s) passed. The Southern Democratic opposition in the Congress to a central route was absent. Previously, railroad company rivalry had prevented the completion of a unified transcontinental route. As the project sponsor, Lincoln had been waiting for this opportunity to initiate the project.

Lincoln was able to see past the Grand Trunk Railroad failure and put the TCR project into perspective. His background as a railroad lawyer gave him insight into how to set up the governance around the project. He saw the war as a testing ground for solving difficult problems facing the project, for example building the total number of bridges (2000). In the fall of 1862, the Construction Corps had experimented with methods of destroying and repairing railroads and bridges. The war had improved railroad technology, created the technical skills to operate complex railroads, created demand that shaped manufacturing capacity in factories, and had a massive impact on procurement of arms, supplies, and materials.

Project Decision #2 Opportunity to Roll the Telegraph into the Project

A second major technology was the wire-telegraph, critical to future communications, which was incorporated into the project by the Act as a subproject. Lincoln was instrumental in this decision as he spent much of his time in a telegraph office sending and receiving telegrams. During the war, 15,000 miles of telegraph cable was laid purely for military purposes. Mobile telegraph wagons reported and received communications from just behind the frontline. Lincoln ran the war on information provided by the telegraph and realised its value and importance.

A multi-wire telegraph system would be constructed alongside the railroad known as the rights of way (In Telegraph, n.d.). The rationale was that the close proximity of telegraph to railroad would make it easier to protect the line, to order more supplies, and to schedule trains for right of way on a single track. This was a major boost to the project business case.

Business Case and Budget

The project had a massive projected cost for which the railroad companies-to-be could not raise the capital. The estimated project cost was a daunting $60m, and so a massive amount of capital investment (over $100m in 1860 dollars) was obtained by selling government guaranteed bonds (granted-per-mile of completed track) and railroad company bonds and stock to interested private investors (Klein 1987).

Lincoln saw how a single line linkage between East and West had a forecast return based on cost savings in military transportation alone of $50 million over 7 years. Also, there was an enormous potential economic impact of opening up the West in trade.

The railroad would open up the West and this expansion would use previously unused or underused land, creating new and taxable wealth. The railroad would also have a political impact of linking the isolated States of California and Oregon and helping them to grow.

This was a public works project that would boost and transform the economy through the demand for products and services. The project required vast quantities of materials that could keep East Coast steel mills at full capacity for many years. In iron materials alone each mile of track required 100 tons of rail, about 2500 ties, and 3 tons of spikes and fish plates and switch mechanisms.

Commercial Relationship, Partnership and Financing

Project Decision #3 to Determine How the Project Is Delivered

At a San Francisco convention in September 1859, a private consortium had engaged the State of California to call upon the national government to initiate a TCR. The consortium was formed by western business leaders the Big Four (led by Theodore Judah, a railroad engineer) who had created the CPRR of California. It was driven by the prospect of tapping into the wealth of the Nevada mining towns, and the forthcoming legislation for federal aid to build the railroad (Bailey 1908).

The Pacific Railroad Act authorised the creation of two competitive railroad companies, CPRR in the west and the UPRR (The Pacific Railroad Act, n.d.) in the east, to build the railroad eastward from Sacramento and westward from Omaha to some meeting point in Utah. It was felt that more than two companies would dilute the resources and reduce their capacity to take on the project. Each company started on either side of the continent so as not to interfere with the other.

Project Decision #4 to Set up the Governance to Direct Railroad Companies

To help drive the project forward the Act governed and directed the companies to compete by using incentives like extensive land grants of alternate sections (1 section = 1 square mile) of government-owned lands along the tracks for 10 miles on both sides of the track. This was based on best practices that had worked for the Illinois Central Railroad (Launius 1965). The land which the grants encompassed was 10% of the entire United States, valued as: 70% valueless desert, 29% good farm or forest land, and 1% had potentially exploitable minerals and very valuable. Government backed bonds ($1000 each over 30-years at 6% interest) were also issued. The two companies were paid $16,000/mile for track laid at level grade, $32,000/mile for track laid in foothills and $48,000/mile for track laid in mountains. This scaled financial incentive evened out any geographic disadvantages. With no agreed midpoint in Utah these incentives encouraged a race to build track quickly.

The central provisions of the act included:

- 10 sections of land grants for every mile of completed railway.
- Companies could use the value of land as collateral for private loans.
- Subsidy bonds, a second mortgage, to lend funds to companies.
- Loans to be repaid by transportation revenues and land sales.
- The government to receive non-monetary benefits (e.g. troop transport cost reductions).
- Increased financial returns by 2%.

The project established a Design-Build-Operate model (Kwak & Chic 2009) where the private sector was not responsible for the project financing but for the design, construction, operation and maintenance of a project for a specified period prior to handing it over to the public sector.

Improving the Business Case with New Growth

Project Decision #5 to Encourage the Building of Towns Along the Route

It was unlikely that the railroads to the thinly populated west would repay the project for a long time. Lincoln saw the railroad as an opportunity to encourage settlers to move out west beyond the crowded Eastern cities.

The 1862 Homestead Act was passed (after the Railroad Act) whereby settlers could claim public lands (160 acres was called a homestead) for a small fee; by living on the land for 5 years the title would become vested in them. This was another substantial potential benefit of the project and addition to the business case. The railroad would provide safe and dependable transportation for the settlers to move west. Furthermore, union soldiers could deduct their years of service from the 5-year residency requirement. The railroads would make money twice by transporting people, goods, and commodities for a price, and then by selling portions of their land to arriving settlers (Launius 1965).

Along the route temporary, hell-on-wheels tent towns were created and some became permanent settlements (Klein 1987). Locomotives needed constant water so every 20 miles the companies planted a water-tower and a telegraph station and called it a town. Some of these grew population centres of growth in the new territories. They were very much interlinked to the operation of the railroad and its organic growth.

Scope of the Project and Constraints

The project route was critical as it had a major impact on the project scope.

The principal obstacles were located in the west with the mountain ranges and deserts. The route started in Sacramento, California facing the rugged 7000 feet Sierra Nevada mountains, across the Great Basin and the Nevada desert, onto the Great Salt Lake desert of Utah, and finally the Laramie mountains in Wyoming. In the east the principal obstacles are rivers. Iowa was chosen as the Transfer Depot (mail and goods) where 7 railroads converge (Fig. 4.1).

The original immigrant routes west ran through river valleys, easier for the ox and mule pulled wagons but they were not the best for the railroad to follow because of steep gradients and sharp corners. They also meandered as immigrants sought out water and grass for their animals.

Efforts were made to survey a new, shorter, better route; Sherman's Pass was discovered in 1864. In 1865 a new route was surveyed across Wyoming over 150 miles (240 km) shorter, with a flatter profile, that would be cheaper and easier to construct, and also closer to Denver and the coalfields in the Wasatch and Laramie Ranges.

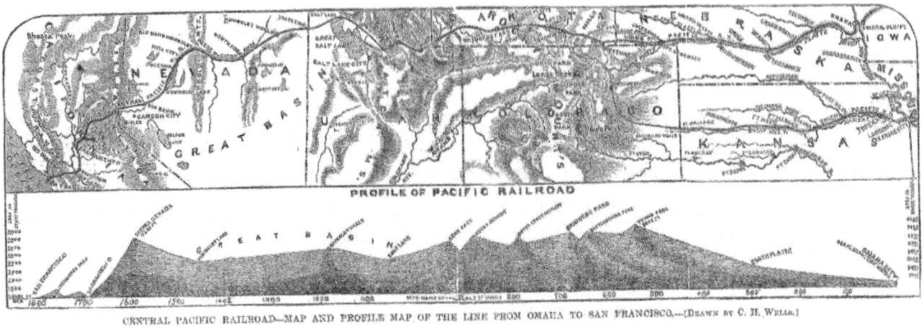

CENTRAL PACIFIC RAILROAD—MAP AND PROFILE MAP OF THE LINE FROM OMAHA TO SAN FRANCISCO.—[DRAWN BY C. H. WELLS.]

Fig. 4.1 Highlights in 2 views the geography and obstacles on the route of the TCR (*Harper's Weekly* December 7, 1867)

Project Supply Chain

Project Decision #6 to Use the Project to Boost the Economy as It Required Vast Quantities of Materials

The railroad required an enormous amount of tools, materials and supplies including locomotives, wheel trucks, rolling stock, machinery and foundry tools. All these had to be shipped from eastern mills to Atlantic ports and loaded onto vessels. The project supply chain was extensive as shipping these materials to San Francisco involved an 18,000 mile journey around Cape Horn, an expensive and hazardous 8 months with obstacles, risks and hardships. The Panama Railroad (1855) shortened the journey considerably and was in operation but freight rates were double that of the Cape Horn trip Everything had to be ordered well in advance and included anything that would sell at a profit like groceries, alcohol, clothing, boots, tools, hardware, furniture, knocked-down houses (for reassembly), medicines and seeds. Materials were also shipped for the wire-telegraph sub-project that included telegraph poles, wire and insulators in large quantities. Up to 30 ships were needed for this supply chain. From San Francisco everything was transferred to river steamers that travelled upriver to Sacramento, and then offloaded onto horse-drawn wagons which travelled to the rail head. Eventually platform cars replaced these wagons as trains become operational.

Project Decision #7 Introduce Standards for a Consistent Approach

The Act of 3 March 1863 (12 Sta. 807) established the gauge of the Pacific railroad and its branches throughout the whole network, from the Pacific coast to the Missouri river, four feet and eight and one-half inches. As we have seen, this had previously been established by George Stephenson in England for the SDR project and later for the Liverpool and Manchester Railway (1830) and was already popular with railroads in the Northeastern states. A common gauge allowed easy transfer of cars between different railroad companies and facilitated trackage rights between companies.

Decision—CPRR Use Local Materials

Project Decision #8 to Use Local vs Imported Materials Timber/Stone Where Possible & Keep Costs Down

An approach to scope reduction is the use and reuse of local materials. One critical decision was to increase the volume of timber used in the construction by using wooden trestle bridges.

CPPR broke ground on January 8, 1863 and progress along the Sacramento Valley was rapid with the use and reuse of local materials. Timbers cut from California forests for ties, bridges and trestles were of a quality that required no special treatment, and also provided fuel for locomotives. Stone of good quality was available through the mountains on the route for culverts, bridge piers and foundations, whilst coarse sands and gravels washed down in creeks was used for ballast. For the UPRR there weren't such ready materials:

> Water was scarce after leaving the Truckee & Humboldt Rivers… There was not a tree that would make a board on over 500 miles of the route, no satisfactory quality of building stone. The country afforded nothing. Lewis Metzler Clement. (CPPR FAQ, n.d.)

Project Adjustments—Sub-Projects Snow Sheds

Project Decision #9 Snow Slides & Avalanches Serious Problem—Cost Both in Lives (with Scores of Men Lost) and Labour

Progress along the Sacramento Valley was rapid but soon slowed at the Sierra Nevada Mountains with the winter snowstorms; this was CPRR's greatest and most underestimated problem. The track was shovelled by half of the work force (9000 men) who suffered from pneumonia and frostbite. Inadequate shelter from avalanches caused scores of deaths (Black Powder, n.d.).

In response, a sub-project was initiated to keep the project going and the tracks operational during the long winters. The workforce constructed enclosed wooden snow sheds (John Debo Galloway 1950) which extended the slope of the mountain so avalanches could pass over the shed roof. Workers were better protected, and the project could continue. A total of 37 miles of snow sheds were needed and the sub-projected lasted three years at a cost of $2m. *Those snow sheds will pay for their cost in a single winter.* E. B. Crocker (legal counsel) (Snow Sheds, n.d.).

This is a good example of a project opportunity opening up, based on adjusting requirements according to unforeseen risk, as the building of snow sheds was not in the initial plan.

Impact of the Civil War on the Project

The intensification of the war created competition for railroad materials (rails, ties, locomotives) and workers used in repairing the damaged rail networks. This caused raging inflation which had a substantial impact on the project as both equipment and labour became difficult to acquire. The price of one ton of rails increased from $55 to $115, and one keg of black powder increased from $2.50 to $15. Progress was slow on the project during the war years (1861–1865).

Decision—Adjusting the Project Governance

Project Decision #10 1864 Railroad Act Adjusts Project & Modifies Approach of the Companies to Align to Project Charter

The 1864 Railroad Act (The Pacific Railroad Act, n.d.) was passed to encourage competition between the two companies and speed up the project specifically in the East and addressed several problematic issues. The Act doubled the available capital of the previous Act (1862) and ceded all natural resources on the line to the 2 companies. It removed limitations on individual stock ownership and issued new stock in shares of $100–$1000 and increased the number of shares to one million from 100,000. It regulated the taking of private property for right of way. It increased land granted from 10 to 20 miles on both sides of the track. The time was extended to one year for filing with the government a designated a route and map for completing track. Provisions were made for UPRR to obtain a proportion of government bonds for work in the mountains.

Haupt's Experimentation and Laboratory

During the war the Union Army engineers and surveyors kept the trains running and tracks maintained. Led by Herman Haupt they set up the Construction Corps which had mastered rapid bridge reconstruction and put back into operation rail lines/bridges that had been destroyed, including seized Confederate lines. The war had already highlighted the effectiveness of the railroad with spectacular shifts of large army units from one strategic field to another. A remarkable example was the movement of General Hooker's two corps of 22,000 men over 1200 miles from Virginia to Chattanooga. Both armies were supported and transported by extensive rail networks which were under constant repair as the armies advanced and retreated. At the end of the war in 1865 Haupt's Corps had grown from 300 men in 1863 to nearly 10,000, and the Union Army controlled a vast 2000 miles of rail network with a combined rolling stock of 419 engines and 6330 cars, and 2 miles of bridges built or rebuilt, at a cost of nearly $30m. This vast army of men and know how was now available to the TCR project.

The Evolving Project Approach and Solutions

Building rapidly at the lowest initial cost and getting operational became the project mantra and influenced many of the decisions, particularly in selecting technologies. Once in operation and as the railroad became profitable upgrades would be made in railroad equipment (tracks, ties, bridges). Many valleys were bridged by rapidly built temporary wooden trestle bridges, to be replaced later by more permanent structures either solid fill (lower maintenance) or truss bridges. The approach required off-the-shelf, production ready and proven technologies.

Bridges

Project Decision #11 to Determine Types of Bridge and Materials
Over 2000 bridges were required along the route and this had a major impact on the project scope and schedule. The project required a consistent

and repeatable approach to bridge building that was cheap, fast and simple. Arch bridges made from stone or iron require substantial support and are complex to build. The war provided the solution through wooden trestle bridges. During the war the intensity of destruction and reconstruction meant some railroad lines were destroyed and rebuilt as many as 5 times. The war provided best practice experience in rapidly building and rebuilding trestle bridges. Haupt created cutting edge and innovative designs that were simple, quick to construct and durable. The designs enabled workers with little experience to build bridges of any span length and allowed multiple teams to repair different sections of a bridge simultaneously. Standard sizes were used for various components in the bridge structure, and standard construction techniques evolved. When Haupt rebuilt the Potomac Creek Bridge in only 9 rainy days Lincoln observed:

> That man Haupt has built a bridge 400 feet long and 80 feet high, across Potomac Creek, on which loaded trains are passing every hour, and upon my word, gentlemen, there is nothing in it but cornstalks and beanpoles. (Snow 1985)

The project kept advancing bridge limits so that in Wyoming the Dale Creek trestle bridge was 650-foot long and the longest trestle 150 feet high (Ambrose 2001). It swayed in the wind and was terrifying to cross, but it did the job. Preassembled trestle bridges were mass-produced and transported by rail to where repairs or replacement was necessary. The rationale behind this approach was that it reduced cost, schedules and complexity. Later in the project iron truss bridges were used where the truss (supporting sections joined into triangular forms) was manufactured off-site, required fewer supports and was simple to assemble by unskilled workers. Its downward thrust required fewer substantial supports than the horizontal thrust of an arch bridge (Bain 2000).

Tunnels

Project Decision #12 to Resort to Tunnels in the Mountains
Deep into the Sierra Nevada Mountains the CPRR project was blocked by massive, granite ridges. The project approach was to build tunnels and cut-throughs based on the goal of limiting the railroad gradients to 2 degrees. Although tunnels are difficult to build, they would considerably shorten the length of the railway and were free of snow. Throughout the entire

project 19 tunnels were built (CPRR build 15, and UPRR 4). The longest is the Summit at 1750 feet long going through solid granite, and at an elevation of 7000 feet. Workers wielding hammers and chisels make the holes into which blasting powder was packed. All tunnels were worked on from both sides simultaneously till they met in the middle.

Cut-Throughs

Project Decision #13 to Resort to Cut-Throughs in the Mountains
In areas where the gradient was too steep, cut-throughs were blasted out. This is highly dangerous work but relatively rapid. Up to 500 kgs of powder were used a day (California Powder Works, 2018). The debris was hauled out with small horse carts and used as fill to elevate the railroad bed. In 1864 The Bloomer Cut was completed in months and, at 63 feet deep and 800 feet long, was hailed as the Eighth Wonder of the World.

UPRR Progress Is Late and Corruption Occurs

During the war years UPRR found it difficult to obtain financial backing, and to organise railroad workers and supplies. They put out a tender for the building of one hundred miles of the railroad, and in August 1864 Herbert M. Hoxie won the bid. He then signed the contract over to the Vice President of Union Pacific T. C. Durant who then passed it onto his new company, Credit Mobilier (Klein 1987) which generated giant profits. This allowed Durant to pay himself illegally for construction, without congressional oversight. In 18 months, Mobilier's shares increased in value by 341%.

When the war ended the project incorporated the supply chain created by the war. Thousands of discharged soldiers (Union and Confederate) of all races were recruited by UPRR as semi-skilled workers as were many engineers from Haupt's Corps who had learned their trade keeping the trains running during the War (Collins 2010). Construction by UPPR started in July 1865, but by year end only 40 miles of track was laid and $500,000 spent for 'two streaks of rust across the Nebraska prairie' as one newspaper said.

To supply one mile of track with materials and supplies required about forty rail cars, as on the plains everything has to be transported from the Missouri River where the supplies were landed. The supply chain carried rails, ties, bridging, fastenings, all railroad supplies, fuel for locomotives and supplies for the workforce and animals. UPRR's worst problem was finding wood for the railroad ties on Nebraska's nearly treeless prairie.

Finding and Growing a Workforce Out West

Project Decision #14 to Source an Adequate Workforce to Fill the Labour Gaps

The California gold rush created a labour shortage which severely affected the project. To quickly fill the labour gaps the only realistic option was to source an adequate workforce from overseas. In 1865 a large Chinese workforce of 10,000, was drafted (Kraus 1969, p. 49.), that made up 90% of CPRR's workforce for the remainder of the project (Fig. 4.2).

During the winter of 1865–1866, UPRR renewed its efforts and pushed men and supplies as the railroad was constructed rapidly west and a race developed between the two companies. Coal deposits were discovered along the line in Wyoming providing UPRR an advantage.

Innovation Within the Project

The project mantra of build fast, cheap and get operational requires a certain type of project innovation in both process and technology to solve difficult problems. These included negotiating steep gradients through switchbacks and tight curves, pulling a long train over varying gradients, clearing heavy snowfalls or obstacles from tracks and keeping communication lines open. The project required technologies that were proven, off-the-shelf, and could be evolved to be production ready and operational in rugged environments.

Both companies adjusted quickly and efficiently to the immediate environment, became adaptable and innovated new practices. For example, they borrowed from the Swiss who had pioneered railway building in mountainous country with steep gradients. Also, in winter they become proficient in building temporary tracks on ice just to bring in new materials, which were removed before the spring thaw. Complete lines were scrapped when a town offered a financial bonus for switching the tracks through their location.

To negotiate switchbacks and tight curves locomotives were equipped with swivel wheeled trucks. They created greater stability and allowed trains to travel over rough roadbed and high terrain. The 4-4-0 configuration

Fig. 4.2 Chinese labourers at work on the TCR, insourced into the project a reliable and very well organised project workforce on the most challenging parts of the route through the mountains (*Harper's Weekly* December 7, 1867)

(4 wheels on the leading truck and 4 driving wheels, with no trailing truck at the rear) became a standard.

For long trains pulling out of a dead stop, the link and pin couplers allowed too much slack between cars creating a jarring ride. To eliminate this slack between cars, new Miller coupling devices were designed used with shock-absorbing springs to prevent damage from bumping cars. They had greater strength and flexibility to maintain a tight hold over hills, valleys, around curves and rough track.

To manage heavy snowfall conditions state-of-the-art snow ploughs, driven by powerful locomotives, were designed. The lower portion of the plough wedge would scoop up snowdrifts and on the upper-portion, a jutting prow would part the drifts, throwing the snow 60 feet away. To clear track obstacles a new Cow catcher device was designed.

To keep the wire-telegraph operational, improvements were made to the glass insulators to telegraph-wires making them moisture proof. The cementing material (sulphur), saturated with paraffin, had remarkable insulation properties. The blown glass possessed extraordinary properties of repelling moisture.

To increase the progress on building tunnels and cut-throughs the newly invented nitro-glycerine explosive was introduced in 1866 (California Powder Works, 2018). Extremely volatile in its pure, liquid form there were a number of serious accidents in its transportation. Thus, new state regulations prevented its transportation, and CPRR employed a chemist to manufacture it onsite. The progress on tunnels greatly increased from 1.18 to 1.82 feet per day per face as a result (Black Powder, n.d.).

While initially locomotives were imported from Britain, US locomotives were developed that used less expensive cast iron rather than wrought iron for many components to reduce costs. A large number of locomotives were required to get the railroad operational. CPRR ordered 147 locomotives from 9 different suppliers as no single supplier could provide the large orders in 1867/1868 and still service the eastern customers like CPRR. CPRR would have preferred to have fewer suppliers since diversity of locomotives complicated operation and maintenance.

To manage the shipment of locomotives to the west one innovation was to disassemble them into kits of smaller and more manageable packages. This created the opportunity to open up a locomotive factory in the west; in 1867 CPRR opened a repair depot that then turned into locomotive works in Sacramento.

To manage the extremely high cost of material shipment required a reduced out of the box failure rate. Far greater quality control was required at source in the factories before shipment, and this was introduced.

To improve progress in the East UPRR equipped railroad cars as portable bunkhouses for workers with a galley car to prepare meals, bunk cars, and a herd of cows for fresh meat. This gave the workers ready accommodation and hot meals of a higher quality.

Project Completion

Project communication was critical in maximising the impact of the project. The project had to evolve the perceptions of an uninterested public because in the early days of the project the war had all the media attention. However, after the war, as the work on the project accelerated, and prominent men journeyed into the west to see the work, editors all over the country covered the story. This new visibility attracted public attention which continually increased throughout the remainder of the project.

In 1868, with the two companies racing towards each other, newspapers carried daily bulletins of miles laid and vivid descriptions of progress. Public interest started to peak when CPRR crews with 5 train loads of material laid 10 miles of track on a prepared rail bed in one day, a record that still stands today (Heath 1928).

The Golden Spike a ceremonial final spike joins the rails. It was the first nationwide media event. In August 1870 the final connection was made, and the railroad was completed 7 years ahead of schedule (Fig. 4.3).

Corruption

The Credit Mobilier corruption scandal erupted in the press, smearing many established government figures who sold their influence for Credit Mobilier stock. UPRR is bankrupted within 3 years as details surface about Durant's Credit Mobilier overcharging UPPR. Knowingly both companies UPPR and CPPR had realised revenues would take a while:

> The leaders of both companies understood one guiding principle clearly: an unbuilt railroad through unsettled country would not do a profitable business for months, even years, after its completion. Money could be made on the venture not from the railroad itself but from its construction. To do the work, therefore, both groups formed separate construction companies and dominated the management of them as well as the railroad. Under this arrangement, at a time when conflict of interest was still a primitive concept, they in effect made contracts with themselves, taking care to build in generous profits for the construction companies at the expense of the railroad. (Klein 1987)

Corruption was not prevented by the acts that set up the governance to direct the railroad companies.

Fig. 4.3 Highlights the meeting of the locomotives of the Union and Central Pacific lines: The engineers shake hands (*Harper's Weekly*, June 5, 1869)

Project Impact

On Native Americans

Native Americans saw the railroad as a violation of their treaties and some groups raided the labour camps along the line. UPRR increased their security and killed bison, decimating herds which had a devastating effect on Native Americans (King 2012). The railroad connected East and West and accelerated the destruction of what had been in the centre of North America. Many conflicts arose as the railroad project continued westward, and the military was brought into fight Native American tribes. These issues were not considered relevant to the project at the time.

On Commerce, Business and the Economy

In 1860, it took 6 months and $1000 to travel from East to West Coast. After the completion of the TCR, it took 7 days and $65–100. Railroads expanded across the continent once the TCR project proved their economic viability. Railroads were built in northerly and southerly directions, along with new parallel TCRs, the Northern Pacific and Southern Pacific.

The railroad encouraged the growth of US business as the transportation costs of goods plummeted. The transformation achieved in intercontinental trade was substantial with goods produced on a mass scale and rapidly distributed by rail around the country. By 1880 $50 million worth of freight was shipped coast to coast every year. It opened the markets of the west coast and Asia, and it brought the products of eastern industry to the growing populace beyond the Mississippi as new settlers settled on millions of acres of land. Railroads excelled at creating industrial order where no pattern of organisation existed, and this essentially gave access to new territories. The railroad was America's first technology corridor and towns (e.g., Cheyenne and Laramie) along it became railroad or boom towns (Hudson 1982).

The project had a major impact on the expansion of the railroad and steel industries. New industries like Baldwin locomotive works in Philadelphia, rapidly expanded during the war and then become a major supplier to CPRR, and by 1870 had become the largest US locomotive producer.

On the U.S. Population and Culture

The railroad linked people together and movement across the continent was no longer a permanent decision with little chance of a return. Trains carried newspapers, books and people across the continent daily and provided a conduit for ideas and a pathway for discourse where everyone could participate in the same national conversation east or west. The TCR captured the country's imagination.

On Other Projects

The project caused a paradigm shift in railroad building in its ability to conquer massive distances that were previously considered unfeasible. The world viewed railroad technology differently. Observing countries instituted vast railroad building programmes of their own. Following the US lead, Canada completed the Intercolonial railway in 1876 that transformed Canada economically, politically and culturally.

Conclusions

The project changed world perceptions of what could be achieved with rail megaprojects in a number of ways:

- It was 7 years ahead of schedule; incredible for such an ambitious project. To deliver a project early by almost half the initial estimated schedule is practically unheard of in megaprojects (Flyvbjerg 2014).
- It was highly disruptive to an existing market and value network, as it caused transportation costs to plummet. It reshaped views about long-distance land transportation and travel.
- It proved the transformative aspects of TCRs and their impact on all facets of society at all levels, including the economy, population (towns) and culture.
- It moved the scale of railroad building from hundreds to thousands of miles. Both Russia and Canada paid close attention and initiated their own TCRs.

The TCR project was highly successful because of the following elements:

- Governance—Lincoln realised that to complete such a megaproject required commercial relationships and partnerships, supported by financing that was initiated and managed through government acts. The private sector would not have taken on the level of risk involved.
- Risk/opportunity—Lincoln saw the war as a window of opportunity, even though there were huge risks in initiating the project during the war. In 1862 the Union Army developed a unified and efficient railroad network. In contrast the Confederates only understood the usefulness of their railroads in the final war years: historians have attributed this as a significant factor in the loss of the war.
- Innovation—The Union Army innovated railroad technology that is the deployment and project management of technology and not the invention of technology. The army had the resourcing to fund it, the space (non-interference) to experiment (piloting) so that solutions could be found to railroad problems, and the chance to implement and test these. For example, making quick repairs with parts

and materials that work out-of-the-box. All this knowledge was then transferred to the project. The key innovation came in following the project mantra of constructing fast, cheap, and getting operational. This required innovating technologies that could be readily implemented into an environment constrained by harsh climatic and environmental conditions (mountains and deserts), and the rigours of a stupendous 18,000 mile supply chain. The technologies had to be off-the-shelf, adaptable, proven, production ready, work-out-of-the-box, easy to transport, assemble, implement and maintain. The project did not develop a single new invention. But it did innovate and improve many aspects of the technology and develop how the technologies interacted and worked together in extreme conditions.

- Reflexivity—The 1864 Railroad Act demonstrates how closely the government was involved, adjusting the governance of the project-in-flight so as to reinforce the project direction and its outcomes. The act spurred both companies to get into a race. The project had agility and could readjust to incorporate sub-projects like the wire-telegraph, or the snow sheds. The project was reflexive, as in reflecting on what was needed in order to improve, where efforts to survey a new, shorter, better route were continual. This has a major impact both on the scope and cost.
- Transition to Operation—The project was completed quickly and put into operation to generate revenue. The project approach was to get away with the minimum; for example, the Dale Creek Bridge swayed in the wind and was terrifying to cross. But the trains could cross and it was made operational. The railroad operation could then be improved by repairing and replacing known areas of weakness.

Project Management Lessons

The chapter now analyses the case study to draw out lessons of value to contemporary project management. The lessons learnt are of great relevance to contemporary transformation, particularly those concerned with disruptive technology. These include:

Defining a Long-Term Business Case

A business case was established by the Federal Government based on savings in postal services, and military force expenditure. During the project, inflation rapidly escalated costs and put the project in trouble. The business case was readjusted to incorporate settlers and the creation of towns, and this helped mitigate this problem just on cost savings but the economic growth that the towns would generate, and additional taxes collected. It helped maintain the momentum through a very difficult period of the project.

It is important to define a business case that goes beyond the short to medium-term economic results, and that incorporates longer term and more broadly defined benefits with the agility to adjust as new opportunities are presented. Dimitriou et al. (2015) argue that in mega-transport projects it is essential that the long-term benefits are part of the business case. As the project progresses it needs to be continuously reviewed and updated as opportunities are identified. A decision needs to be made on whether these are incorporated into the project and realised but this has an impact on scope.

Role of the Project Sponsor

Lincoln's role was critical in providing a vision, understanding the political landscape, and keeping the project 'alive' when going through the most challenging of times. His industry experience as a railroad lawyer was valuable and gave him insights into the project, as did his experience in the Civil War and understanding of the critical role that Haupt and railroads played. All this gave him the wherewithal to operate proactively and make critical decisions when the project ran into difficulties.

In contemporary project management and digital transformation, roles are changing through the project. The positions responsible for ultimately sponsoring transformation are many and start with the business side. The role of IT is significant and is required not in a servient role but a sponsorship role, to provide a level of leadership to the business because technologies play such a significant overall role in the project.

Projects Are One-Time Opportunities

The unique endeavour was a one-time opportunity because of the astronomical costs and the lack of political opposition because of the civil war. Thus Lincoln through the project had to take advantage of this and initiate the project. Through the project opportunities opened up like the sub-projects for the snow sheds, which helped increase the business case return. A further one-time opportunity was the wire-telegraph which was intertwined with the operation of the railroad but could be used for commercial terms. In addition, it was far easier to support this wire-telegraph route than the existing one which didn't have the same access a railroad provided, and stations along the route.

In contemporary project management and transformation recognising one-time opportunities is critical. The Crossrail project in the UK (Davies et al. 2014) was seen as an incredible one-time opportunity and time to innovate, the previous underground line built in London was the Jubilee in 1979. All along the proposed line 118 km (73 mi) lay opportunities particularly in the centre of London where stations on priceless real-estate could be redeveloped and transport improvements introduced (pedestrian and cyclist facilities) together with a commercial element (piazzas, shopping, apartments).

Setting up the Governance

The commercial relationship and partnership were significant as was the financial (investments) and legal (contracts, land grants, worker's and settlers rights). The Government Acts controlled governance to direct the stakeholders, particularly the railroad companies. The same lessons apply to contemporary transformations, the governance drives the project and behaviour of the stakeholders.

In contemporary project management and transformation, governance is critical to success but needs to be set up at multiple levels starting at a programme level and then within projects. The governance must be able to respond quickly to risk and issue escalations, resolve competing priorities, have the authority to make decisions, make those decisions promptly and monitor programme/project performance. This may be coordinated through a Project Management Office (PMO) that can provide programme and project oversights. The PMO should be attached to the executive office and so to the strategic and tactical business objectives with representation from business and technology and strong relationships to strategic planners, business unit leaders, and the enterprise architecture office, enterprise service owners and vendors. The PMO should be in place over the project duration to deliver the expected outcomes in the expected time frame.

According to Gartner 2017, 'When implemented effectively, program [management] offices can actually reduce overall costs and improve the quality of results through effective management of the interdependencies inherent in transformational programs'.

Fostering Leadership, to Drive Innovation in a Megaproject

Lincolns' experience in the Civil War was critical together with the engineering experience that could be deployed to provide insight into the project and to enable innovation to solve the most critical problems. The entrepreneurial partnerships with commercial companies and with the Chinese government to meet the workforce needs of the project were vital. The railroad company's innovation in many areas in both process and technology solved difficult problems and allowed them to conquer substantial risks and succeed (Kraus 1969). To better understand the types of innovation processes available to a project Salerno et al. (2015) proposed a taxonomy of eight based on the type of project and the project phase where innovation can be introduced. Process #4—public request for a contract, is the best fit for this project as it demonstrates a scenario where in predevelopment an initial analysis of the feasibility of the project is determined that includes the business case and the route surveys. The main activities of the innovation process occur after winning the call and awarding the bid to the two competing companies. The call reduces uncertainty for the companies (developer), who know that there is a market for the project output. This is why public procurement can be an efficient tool for boosting innovation in companies.

Rapidly changing technical and product development skills required by digital transformation projects are rendering traditional strategies for acquiring skills obsolete. Instead, creating external entrepreneurial partnerships is critical. Projects need to be able to build teams with evolving skillsets that keep pace with rapidly changing technologies. Teams are able to rapidly pick up new skillsets through knowledge transfers, leveraging the ecosystems of external companies and partners, co-locations and co-creation of solutions. Any difficulty in acquiring technical and product development skills constrains the project.

Dealing with Uncertainty and Complexity in the Supply Chain

The principal complexities lay with the stakeholders, and with keeping the workforce working at full capacity, with enough materials and equipment available. There were a substantial number of stakeholders across the United States with varied expectations and agendas. An 18,000 mile supply chain using 30 ships had to be coordinated to reach the workforce in time and maintain the project progress.

Dealing with uncertainty and its relationship to project complexity is key. Organisational complexity is particularly common. It can be an issue in mega-projects with the number of hierarchical levels, units, divisions of tasks, etc. Interdependency would be the degree of operational interdependencies between these organisational elements (Baccarini 1996). This differentiation has two dimensions:

- Vertical Differentiation—referring to the depth of the organisational hierarchical structure (the number of levels)
- Horizontal Differentiation—referring to the number of separate formal organisational units, and the division of activities and tasks across these.

Managing this organisational complexity requires introducing various strategies.

Creating a High Morale Culture

According to Kraus (1969) a large Chinese workforce of 10,000 was drafted to quickly fill the labour gaps by the CPRR, attracted by relatively high rates of pay. The incentive for individual workers to travel 5000 miles, was pay of $35/month in gold. Taking into account the work camps they were provided with they could save $20/month; a substantial amount. The workforce was well organised with provision for the health, safety and welfare of the workers including cooks, doctors, laundry services. The diet was healthy (rice, dried fish, fresh vegetables, dried oysters) and drinking tea using boiled water reduced dysentery outbreaks. They had a hard work ethic and wished to return home with good economic gain. This contrasted to Eastern US workers where shanty towns exhibited the worst excesses of alcohol, gambling and brothels.

It has been well established in practice and in the literature from work around the Hawthorne effect (Mayo 1945) that a well-cared for workforce is more productive. Creating a culture with a positive project morale starts with assessing organisational receptiveness and readiness, and an impact assessment of the changes associated with the project/transformation. This then leads to identifying and deploying various strategies to help groups and individuals address the changes. This is kept up through the transformation by proactive communications and by creating a conducive work environment based on the ethical management of a substantial workforce.

Technology Innovation

Haupt's civil war railroad experience gave him insight into the innovation required to solve the most critical problems. Over 2000 bridges and 19 tunnels had to be built, some in extreme and hostile environments; mountains, massive ravines, dense forests and deserts. Many new building practices were evolved from existing processes and techniques. Using both technology (product) and process innovation to create solutions to solving problem of gradients greatly reduced project scope and cost in activities on the critical path. For example, the team adapted swivel wheel trucks which enabled trains to negotiate tight curves and switchbacks to climb steep inclines along mountain routes.

Work on technology innovation, in both products and process, is required to create solutions to solve complex transformation problems. Process innovation can also reduce project scope and cost in activities on the critical path, for example, how rails are laid, or the slope of gradients. For example, one of the primary goals of the Crossrail project (Davies et al. 2014) was to introduce a strategy where the innovation goals were clearly targeted as everyone's responsibility. As Europe's largest engineering construction project, Crossrail had 10,000 workers on more than 40 construction sites. This would create an organisational pathway whereby people from across the supply chain could channel their ideas for innovation, gain the resources required to implement them, and then share these successes across the organisational boundaries that proliferate in megaprojects like Crossrail. The project identified four opportunities for intervening to promote innovation: the bridging, engaging, leveraging and exchanging windows (short periods in the project schedule). Contractors were incentivised to generate new innovation by guaranteeing value created would be shared between client & contractor. In total, 17 firms secured 'Enabling Works Framework Agreements' to compete for packages of works. The Crossrail executive chairman clarified the project's overall strategic approach to innovation that: Innovation is the thing we have to work with—and that will be a partnership between us and the delivery partner and designers to deliver in the most efficient way to produce the best economies (Oliver 2008, p. 6).

Extensive Prototyping and Piloting

Extensive Prototyping and Piloting were required to evolve and adapt emerging technologies for transportation solutions. Herman Haupt's Construction Corps had mastered rapid bridge reconstruction and putting back into operation rail lines/bridges, through experimentation and a laboratory. This was leveraged by the project in many ways, particularly in coming up with new designs for bridges that met the requirements and constraints of the project. Bridge building was a significant project activity with over 2000 bridges required, and the principal constraint was getting materials to site.

In contemporary project management and transformation extensive prototyping and piloting is pivotal when defining new solutions based on the constraints of the project. This is essential to risk mitigation. Piloting allows for failure and helps the project team reflect on the best approaches.

Summary

The TCR provides important lessons for megaprojects in innovation which are not always associated with project management; projects are one-time opportunities and unique endeavours. Sometimes for organisations they may be the only time to innovate as the opportunities may simply not exist after the project. A particular set of circumstances have been explained that allowed the completion of one of the most disruptive projects of the nineteenth century. Effective project management was key to its completion.

References

Ambrose, Stephen E. (2001), *Nothing Like It in the World: The Men Who Built the Transcontinental Railroad, 1863–1869.* New York: Simon & Schuster.

Baccarini, D. (1996), The concept of project complexity—A review. *International Journal of Project Management* 14: 201–204. https://doi.org/10.1016/0263-7863(95)00093-3.

Bailey, W. (1908), The Story of the Central Pacific. Retrieved from http://cprr.org/Museum/Bailey_CPRR_1908.html.

Bain, D.H. (2000), Pride and Pitfalls Along a Coast to Coast Track, by Michael Kenney. *Boston Globe*, January 10. A book review: Empire Express: Building the First Transcontinental Railroad.

Carlos, Ann M., and Lewis, Frank D. (1995), The Creative Financing of an Unprofitable Enterprise: The Grand Trunk Railway of Canada, 1853–1881. *Explorations in Economic History* 32 (3): 273–301.

Collins, R.M. (2010), *Irish Gandy Dancer: A tale of building the Transcontinental Railroad.* Seattle: Create Space. ISBN 978-1-4528-2631-8.

Davies, A., MacAulay, S., DeBarro, T., and Thurston M. (2014), Making Innovation Happen in a Megaproject: London's Crossrail Suburban Railway System. *Project Management Journal* 45 (6): 25–37.

Dimitriou, H., Ward, E.J., and Wright, P.G. (2015), *Lessons for Mega Transport Project Developments and the Future of UK Cities and Regions.* Retrieved from https://assets.publishing.service.gov.uk/government/uploads/system/uploads/attachment_data/file/499051/future-of-cities-mega-transport-projects.pdf.

Flyvbjerg, B. (2014), What You Should Know About Megaprojects and Why: An Overview. *Project Management Journal* 45 (2): 6–19.

Heath, E. (1928), A Railroad Record That Defies Defeat: How Central Pacific Laid Ten Miles of Track in One Day Back in 1869. *Southern Pacific Bulletin* XVI (5): 3–5. Retrieved February 15, 2019, from http://cprr.org/Museum/Southern_Pacific_Bulletin/Ten_Mile_Day.html.

Hudson, J. (1982), Towns of the Western Railroads. *Great Plains Quarterly* 2 (Winter): 41–54.

Hutchison, C. (2015), *A History of American Civil War Literature.* Cambridge: Cambridge University Press.

Galloway, C.E., John Debo. (1950), *The First Transcontinental Railroad.* New York: Simmons-Boardman, Ch. 7.

King, G. (2012), Where the Buffalo No Longer Roamed. Retrieved February 15, 2019, from https://www.smithsonianmag.com/history/where-the-buffalo-no-longer-roamed-3067904/.

Klein, M. (1987), Book Union Pacific: The Birth of a Railroad 1862–1893. University of Minnesota Press, pp. 100–101. KPMG's Global Transformation Study (2016), Succeeding in disruptive times. Retrieved from https://assets.kpmg.com/content/dam/kpmg/pdf/2016/05/global-transformation-study-2016.pdf.

Kraus, G. (1969), Chinese Laborers and the Construction of the Central Pacific. *Utah Historical Quarterly* 37 (1) (Winter): 41–57. PDF Copyright Utah State Historical Society, used by permission. Retrieved January 21, 2019, from http://cprr.org/Museum/Chinese_Laborers.html.

Launius, R. (1965), The Railroads and the Space Program Revisited: Historical Analogues and the Stimulation of Commercial Space Operations. *Astropolitics* 12 (2–3): 167–179.

Mayo, E. (1945), *Social Problems of an Industrial Civilization.* Boston: Division of Research, Graduate School of Business Administration, Harvard University, p. 72.

Oliver, A. (2008). Doug on the dig. Douglas Oakervee interview. Building Crossrail: Major Project Report. *New Civil Engineer* November, 4–6.

Salerno et al. (2015), Innovation Processes: Which Process for Which Project? *Technovation* 35: 59–70.

Snow, R. (1985), Herman Haupt. *American Heritage* 36 (2) (February/March): 54–55.

No Author

'Black Powder and Nitroglycerine on the Transcontinental Railroad', n.d. Article. Retrieved February 14, 2019, from https://railroad.lindahall.org/essays/innovations.html.

'CPPR FAQ', n.d. CPRR Museum Article. Retrieved February 14, 2019, from https://cprr.org/Museum/FAQs.html.

'The Pacific Railroad Act of 1862 (12 Stat. 489) was the original act. Some of its provisions were subsequently modified, expanded, or repealed by four additional amending Acts: The Pacific Railroad Act of 1863 (12 Stat. 807), Pacific Railroad Act of 1864 (13 Stat. 356), Pacific Railroad Act of 1865 (13 Stat. 504), and Pacific Railroad Act of 1866 (14 Stat. 66)', n.d. Wiki Article. Retrieved September 6, 2018, from https://en.wikipedia.org/wiki/Pacific_Railroad_Acts.

'Snow Sheds: How the CPRR Crossed the Summit', n.d. Article. Retrieved February 14, 2019, from https://railroad.lindahall.org/essays/innovations.html.

'In Telegraph: Development of the Telegraph Industry', n.d. Britannica Article. Retrieved January 26, 2019, from https://www.britannica.com/technology/telegraph#ref607719.

CHAPTER 5

Chapter Case Study 3: The Manchester Ship Canal and the World's First Industrial Park

Abstract This project turned a landlocked city into a commercial seaport. More importantly this infrastructure transitioned the city commercially from a cotton production centre to a diversified manufacturing centre through Britain's first industrial estate based on the technologies (electricity, combustion engine) and processes (production-line, verticalisation, mass-production) of the second industrial revolution replacing those of the first industrial revolution (steam). The local economy rapidly grew and the city became an economic powerhouse. Because of opposition the realisation of the canal took much longer and arrived when competitive transportation costs in rail had plummeted. However, the project had the foresight to recognise emerging opportunities, and address these. Industrial parks were a new concept that required the right conditions and infrastructure, and the canal and docks catalysed this.

Keywords Project sponsor role · Defining business case · Exploiting unexpected opportunities · Governance · Uncertainty and complexity

Introduction

The Manchester Ship Canal (1887–1894) (MSC) was arguably one of the most significant transformation projects of the nineteenth century in the UK. The construction of the commercial canal, initially delayed by

M. Kozak-Holland and C. Procter, *Managing Transformation Projects*, https://doi.org/10.1007/978-3-030-33035-4_5

political and economic opposition, was a first in turning a landlocked city (Manchester is 36 miles [58 kms] from the coast) into a seaport and was significant in proving the viability of such a project. More importantly it helped Manchester transition commercially from a cotton production centre to a diversified manufacturing sector through Britain's first industrial estate, Trafford Park, established by the canal and docks. It established a manufacturing centre based on the technologies (electricity, combustion engine) and processes (production-line, verticalisation, mass-production) of the second industrial revolution replacing those of the first industrial revolution (steam). It led to the rapid growth of the local economy and became a major centre for weapons production in WW1 and WW2.

Inspired by the Suez Canal (1859–1869), it was arguably the largest infrastructure project in the UK in the late nineteenth century, with a workforce of 12,000 and 200 steam trains hauling 6000 wagons. At the heart of the project was the commitment of the project owner and their partnerships with other commercial entities and the public sector in Manchester Corporation. The completion of the project involved addressing numerous unique obstacles including technical, legal and financial conflicts. Despite these, the project met its specifications, was completed on schedule but did not come within budget. This entrepreneurial partnership and leadership stepped into the project to complete it. More importantly it led to the setting up of an industrial park that was truly transformative of the local and UK economy, and set up a model for industrial growth copied globally.

This case study is set in the context of a substantial and growing body of knowledge examining transformation projects, and contemporary research into long-term effects of transformations through effective project partnerships. The lessons of failure and success from the MSC project are of considerable relevance to today's transformation projects.

The textual evidence concerning the construction of the MSC is reliable as the megaproject had significant exposure in local and national media. Today there are many first-hand accounts of people involved and newspapers that covered the project.

Background—The History of UK Canal Building

Canals had existed for over 4000 years and had proved to be an effective means of transportation. Manchester, a landlocked city, had a booming cotton economy that required a transportation system to move product around the world. In the 1820s the monopolistic rates charged by canal (barge) between Manchester and Liverpool started an agitation which led directly to the construction of a railway between the two cities. Charges imposed on Manchester companies for the use of Liverpool's docks and the connecting railway had created an atmosphere of resentment within the business community. There had been occasional proposals as early as 1840 (Leech 1907) for a sea canal. By the mid-1870s Manchester's supply lines were being stretched to their limits. Goods could often be imported and bought from the Port of Hull, on the other side of country, at a cheaper rate than via Liverpool. In the 1880s the high railway tariff between the cities caused considerable agitation (Moulton 1910).

> "I am told by railway men that there is no traffic in the country worked at a lower cost than the traffic between Manchester and Liverpool, and yet we pay the highest rate of carriage in the kingdom." Sir William Forwood. (Leech 1907)

With the objective to give the landlocked industrial manufacturing sector in Manchester direct access to the sea, proposals had been submitted for an ocean canal as early as 1840, but the costs were always prohibitive.

Project Initiation

Manchester had been built on manufacture of cotton using water transportation, where canals were a key part of the infrastructure Maw et al. (2012). However, by 1880 Manchester cotton business owners were trying to solve the problem of transporting large volumes of cotton around the world. Although Liverpool was the second largest UK port, high railway tariffs drove them in 1882, to form a provisional committee to endorse the project and raise a fund for the purpose of defraying the necessary expenses incident to the securing of a charter from Parliament.

To prove the case for a ship canal, adequate for ocean-going vessels from Manchester to the sea, was not easy for the committee as stiff and determined opposition developed on the part of the railways, the Mersey Docks and Harbour Board, the Liverpool Corporation, and the owners of great estates. According to Moulton (1910, p. 450):

> In the parliamentary sessions of 1883-85 no less than 175 days were consumed in the discussion of the project. Witnesses were cross-questioned as in a criminal trial, and their statements and statistics were subjected to the most

> searching criticism. As many as 326 petitions in favour of the project were presented by cities, chambers of commerce, and trading and manufacturing companies of the district interested.

It was only after three years of persistent effort on the part of the project sponsors that led to a parliamentary sanction and the authorising Act for the canal was finally passed in 1885.

The concept of a ship canal was not new; there was previous project experience in constructing ship canals based on a ship's depth, width and length. These included Suez 1869, Amsterdam-North Sea (1866–1872) £4.9 million, work done on the Clyde and the Tyne, where good ports were practically made from shallow rivers. The failure of the first Panama Canal project (1881–1889) by the French had highlighted the risks in building an 80 km canal and importance of understanding the geography and topology, and the impact of weather and climate.

Evolving Vision

In another, though indirect, manner it was hoped that the canal would reward the expenditures of its builders. It was believed that in addition to building up huge traffic by water, and securing for all time low transportation charges, the Manchester Ship Canal would attract many new industries to the region. The report of the committee of 1886 expressed the conviction that along the entire length of the canal great manufacturing establishments would be erected, that ship-building would become a great industry on the banks of the canal, and that Warrington, Runcorn, and other intermediate cities between Manchester and Liverpool would quickly become thriving commercial ports (Moulton 1910).

Scope of the Project and Constraints

A contract was entered into with Messrs. Lucas & Aird to execute the work for £5.75 million and they agreed to pay 4%, interest on capital during construction. Thomas Walker was appointed as contractor and Edward Leader Williams, a civil engineer was the lead designer of the Canal. He helped the Manchester Ship Canal Company formulate its proposals for the necessary Act of Parliament. The first construction work started in November 1887 (Leech 1907).

Project Decision #1 Resolve 70 Feet Elevation Above Sea-Level

The 70 foot elevation of Manchester above the sea-level required a solution as to whether to lower the docks or raise the height of the canal by 70 feet. The latter would necessitate a complex lock system. This was the first major decision and was based on cost and water supply, where the locks would have to be fed by rivers. As a result, five sets of gigantic locks were proposed which were to be positioned at key junctures with rivers.

Project Decision #2 to Build a Sea Retaining Wall

At Runcorn and the Mersey Estuary, where the River Mersey is narrow, a degree of protection was required against rapid erosion of walls by the sea. This necessitated a concrete sea-wall 4300 feet long to support the embankment and offer a degree of protection. The huge sea wall had to rise in places from a depth of 40 feet, and average 12 feet in thickness, and required over one million cubic yards of stone in the wall.

Project Decision #3 Relates to the Existing Transportation Infrastructure Canal and Rail

This major decision related to the proposed route of the canal cutting across existing transportation lines and the infrastructures of existing rails, roads and canals, namely the Bridgewater Canal. This required complex and sophisticated engineering solutions as these transportation infrastructures need to remain intact and operational throughout the project without interruption. Options included:

- Tunnels, like the Severn Tunnel, which are costly and difficult to build and often requiring permanent pumping power.
- High elevation bridges which are costly to construct and require a shallow gradient that requires much land and space.
- Swing bridges which are both dangerous and inconvenient but have a much smaller footprint and shorter construction time.

This resulted in agreement to build the following solutions:

The Bridgewater Canal would be crossed by a swing bridge and its course stopped and swung at right angles during the passage of large ships. The structure would be moved by hydraulic power; the weight of the movable portion, including the water, was 1600 tons. An alternative scheme using a double lock flight was rejected, because of the need to conserve water in the Bridgewater Canal above (Ryall 2000). The new aqueduct would be designed by Edward Leader Williams and built by Andrew Handyside and the Company of Derby. The weight of the structure meant that the design would be pushing the limits of the possible. This would be the first and only swing aqueduct in the world and considered a major feat of Victorian civil engineering.

There are nine main roads across the canal, all requiring swing bridges; those below Barton have to clear a span of waterway 120 feet. The width of these bridges would vary from 20 feet to 36 feet, and they would be constructed of steel, their weight varying from 500 to 1000 tons each. They work on a live ring of conical cast-iron rollers, and are moved by hydraulic power supplied by steam, gas or oil engines. The Trafford Road Bridge at the Manchester Docks was the heaviest swing bridge on the canal: with extra width it weighed 1800 tons.

There were five existing railways lines that had to be crossed and this was important, both to the travelling public and the canal traders. The main line of the London and North-Western to Scotland was, perhaps, the most important one that had to be crossed. Eventually to facilitate construction high-level deviation lines were adopted for each railway crossing the canal.

Project Decision #4 Relates to the Harbour, and Docks Infrastructure

The canal required extensive docks, storage sheds and other necessary equipment to run a full transportation operation. Loading and unloading of ships, movement of goods in and out of storage had to be efficient and quick.

The decision made, with an eye on the future, was to build a magnificent set of nine docks, on a grand scale. There was also a solid concrete and steel shed, half a mile long and three stories in height, and a huge grain elevator with a capacity of 1,500,000 bushels (12 m gallons), equipped with the most modern improvements. The area of the docks was 104 acres, with 152 acres of quay space, having over 5 miles of frontage to the docks, which are provided with a number of three storey transit sheds, thirteen seven storey and seven four storey warehouses and a large grain silo.

A railway network ran through the industrial estate covering 26 route miles (42 km), and inland canals connected the docks.

Project Decision #5 Approach Dictated by Topology and Geology

The builders of the canal were exceptionally fortunate in the matter of construction materials. Suitable filling-in material was plentiful along the entire route, while rock, clay, and sand for the making of the sea wall embankments were found in abundance. The clay embankments would be faced with heavy coursed stone on each side.

Project Execution

As many men were employed on the works as could be obtained, but the number never exceeded 17,000, and the greater part of the excavation was done mechanically by about eighty steam navies (diggers) and land dredgers. For the conveyance of excavations and materials, 228 miles of temporary railway lines were laid, and 173 locomotives, 6300 wagons and trucks and 316 fixed and portable steam engines and cranes were employed, at a total cost of approx. £1,000,000 (Leech 1907).

Project Decision #6 Organisation of Workforce to Work in Parallel

The project workforce was organised to work in parallel by subdividing the 36 mile route of the canal into eight separate sections, with a civil engineer responsible for each stretch and its team.

Project Construction

At Eastham, six miles south east of Liverpool in the mouth of the Mersey river, the entrance locks to the Manchester Ship Canal were constructed. These locks were tidal for vessels up to 15,000 tons deadweight capacity. At each lock system a pumping installation was built which enabled the successive levels to be maintained from the sea (Fig. 5.1).

The building of a sea retaining wall and the lock system were substantial project activities.

Project Decision #7 Construction Railway Followed the Canal

A temporary railway was set up for the construction following the route of the former River Irwell to bring in construction materials. Every month this allowed more than 10,000 tons of coal and 8000 tons of cement to be

Fig. 5.1 The building of the Manchester Ship Canal 1889, Manchester Docks Section through 4 views. Much excavation was done mechanically with steam navies and land dredgers (Grace's Guide Collection)

delivered to sites along the canal excavation. This improved the efficiency and saved costs.

Project Decision #8 to Initiate Substantial Repair Work Following Unexpected Flooding and Cold Winter

Initially the construction work went well, and all schedules were met, but in November 1889 the lead contractor Walker died. Further delays were caused by bad weather and repeated flooding from rivers that caused serious setbacks (November 1890 and December 1891) and great damage to the slopes of the canal. In all 23 miles of the unfinished canal had to be pumped out before the construction work was completed. Red sandstone seemed at first very good rock but when depended upon as a wall to the canal it proved inadequate and turned out to be laminated by veins of sand, giving way under the action of water and weather. The brick-work to fix defects was an unexpected addition to the project cost. For a long period of time over 450,000 bricks per week were produced as needed right along the side of the construction works (Moulton 1910, p. 461).

The costs were further impacted when the Bridgewater Canal, the Company's only source of income, was closed after a fall of ice (Owen 1983).

Project Decision #9 Arbitration Leads to Significant Delays in Rebuilding Bridges

The Manchester Ship Canal Company also decided to take over the contracting work and bought all the on-site equipment for £400,000 (Owen 1983, p. 53). Some railway companies, whose bridges had to be modified to cross the canal, demanded compensation. The London and North Western Railway and Great Western Railway refused to cooperate, and between the rail companies they demanded about £533,000 for inconvenience. The Company was unable to demolish the older, low railway bridges until August 1893, when the matter went to arbitration. The railway companies were awarded just over £100,000, a fraction of their combined claims (Owen 1983).

Project Decision #10 to Stave off Project Shutdown and Bankruptcy of Consortium

By early 1891, the Company had exhausted its capital of £8 million in 4 years, with only half the construction work completed (Willan 1977, p. 174) and they were forced to seek financial help from the Manchester Corporation in order to avoid bankruptcy. The required funds were approved and released by the Corporation in March that year, in order to 'preserve the city's prestige' and the project was completed. The cost to Manchester Corporation had a significant impact on local taxpayers and the municipal debt rose by 67%, leading to a 26% increase in rates (i.e., local taxes) between 1892 and 1895 (Willan 1977, p. 174).

Project Implementation

More than 41,000,000 m^3 of material were excavated, about half as much as was removed during the building of the Suez Canal (Farnie 1980). The ship canal opened on the 1st January 1894 when 71 vessels made the 36 mile journey.

Project Outcome

The completion of the project involved addressing numerous unique obstacles including political (opposition from Liverpool, the railway owners), technical (the Bridgewater Canal had to be carried over the canal), environmental (flooding) and financial (resolved through the partnership with Manchester Corporation).

The expenditure on the works, including plant and equipment, to 1 January 1900, was £10,327,666. The purchase included all of the Mersey and Irwell and Bridgewater Canal Navigations, £1,786,651. Land and compensation, £1,223,809. Interest on capital during construction, £1,170,733. These items together with parliamentary and general expenses bring up the total cost of the canal to £15,248,437.

Moulton (1910, p. 452) begins by stating the project was a success:

> Competition has forced down the rates charged by the railways, while the canal borne traffic travels at a still lower cost. Distributing business has been built up in Manchester, and the relative decline of the city has been checked in no small degree. The trans-shipping business alone furnishes a large amount of employment, and, in addition, new industries have developed on the canal. All this means more business and larger opportunity for the people of Manchester, whose splendid enterprise has brought the sea in-land to the very centre of their business activities.

Despite being 36 miles from the sea, the Manchester Ship Canal allowed the newly founded Port of Manchester to establish itself as the third busiest port in the UK and would transform the city economically and socially.

Project Success or Failure

Moulton (1910, p. 452) revises his view of the project success based on the large project costs and the slow payback:

> A careful first-hand investigation of the entire project has, however, led the writer to the conclusion, that the Manchester Ship Canal has fallen far short of fulfilling the expectations of its builders, and that, splendid engineering achievement as it is, its economic advantages are of very questionable importance. In the first place, the canal cost more than twice the amount of the original estimate.

The chief engineer, finding himself utterly unable to complete the work under double the amount of his bid, gave up in despair, and the work had to be finished by others taking over the position. Expenditures kept mounting higher and higher, and it became necessary for the Company to borrow an extra £5,000,000 from the city of Manchester in order to finish the work.

The cost of the technical solutions was high with the only swing aqueduct in the world, 9 swing bridge roads, sea walls, locks and extensive docks well beyond the expected budget. The Company took over contracting work and bought all the on-site equipment. It also got itself into a dispute with railway companies over compensation for railway bridges that had to go to arbitration.

Even 16 years after the project the Company had not been able to meet in full the interest on the £5,000,000 loan. Moulton summarised that the two reasons for this failure to pay dividends were excessive expenditures, and small traffic.

But it frequently did not work out that the rate from Liverpool to Manchester by canal, plus the railway charge from Manchester to some other UK city was less than from Liverpool to this point direct by rail, especially when the delays and inconveniences of the canal route were considered.

The Unexpected? Catalyst to Further Transformation Opportunities

The canal was slow to generate the predicted volume of traffic. A successful businessman called Ernest Terah Hooley (the Chairman of Schweppes, Raleigh Cycles, Dunlop Tyres and Bovril) bought an island estate along the canal for £360K. He planned to make a new golf course, a race course and new super dwellings for the wealthy.

Hooley formed Trafford Park Estates Ltd., transferring his ownership of the park to the new Company—of which he was the chairman and a significant shareholder—at a substantial profit. Marshall Stevens was the manager of the new Ship Canal Company and he set out to persuade Hooley that he was sat on a major opportunity. If factories were built alongside the new canal, then Liverpool's docking fees could be avoided. Ships could load and unload in the Salford Docks, by-pass Liverpool and sail directly into the Irish Sea—the gateway to the World. Hooley liked this new idea and Trafford Park Estates was opened on the 17 August 1896 with Marshall

Stevens as the new general manager. The world's first industrial park, Trafford Park, was established offering businesses world-wide many facilities but greatest of all, a rail system from the dockside to their new factory free with access to the 15,000 ton ships or the main railway system of Britain.

The turn of the twentieth century was on the cusp of a transition into the second industrial revolution driven by new emerging technologies of electricity, and petroleum with general purpose technologies (dynamo, electric motor, combustion engine [Carlsson 2004]). In the United States these technologies were driving changes in industry; manufacturers and US industrialists looking for a base in the UK were interested in Trafford Park. Trafford Park's board encouraged diversity in the goods being manufactured on their estate. In contrast to textile-dominated central Manchester, Trafford Park's formative years embraced steel foundries, biscuit factories, oil works and cars.

G. Westinghouse was extremely interested in electricity and alternating current machines; he already had 5 factories in America. He made a reconnaissance of Britain in the 1890s and opened a small factory in London. The Trafford Park advertisement greatly intrigued him, and he decided to invest there. He was told that the factory he required would take 5 years to build. He refused to accept this and sent for his own American gang of civil engineers. The proud British brickies who could lay 400 bricks per day were put on a crash course and learned to lay 2000 bricks per day. He increased the labour force fivefold and built everything in 18 months at a cost of £1.25m. In 1903, manufacturing began, and 3000 men were employed and nearly 1000 women. Westinghouse also built a village for his workers (Trafford Park, n.d.).

In 1903, the Cooperative Wholesale Society (CWS), bought land at Trafford Wharf and set up a large food-packing factory and a flour mill (Nicholls 1996). Other companies arriving at about the same time included Kilverts (lard manufacturers), the Liverpool Warehousing Company, and Lancashire Dynamo & Crypto Ltd.

Ford's Significant Entry to Trafford Park and Ushering in the Second Industrial Revolution

In 1911, Ford acquired a disused carriage works/tram factory at the Trafford Park industrial zone near Manchester and opened its first factory outside of the United States employing 60 people. They established a Model T assembly plant at Trafford Park because of its proximity to the Manchester Ship Canal. Originally it was established merely to assemble vehicles using parts imported from their Dearborn, Detroit factory in the United States (Ford of Britain 1968). But the distances complicated the assembly process, and significantly added to the production cost so the plant quickly took to purchasing components on its own account closer to home.

Back in 1908, Ford first used the recent industrial trends of an assembly line and interchangeable parts in order to assemble a car more quickly than anyone had done before. Breaking the assembly of the Model T into 84 distinct steps the workforce was divided, where each worker was trained to do just one of these steps (Ford installs, n.d.). Ford had in effect invented assembly line auto-production (Carlsson 2004) and the company's innovative production-line method was introduced at roughly the same time at Trafford Park as in Dearborn, giving the British factory an opportunity to observe and progressively introduce this new technique. Between 1912 and 1913 output at Trafford Park more than doubled from 3000 to 7000 cars pa, as the moving-chassis assembly line was introduced.

At the end of 1913 Ford was the leading UK producer, building 7310 cars that year, followed by Wolseley at 3000, Humber (making cars since 1898 in Coventry) at 2500, Rover (Coventry car maker since 1904) at 1800 and Sunbeam (producing cars since 1901) at 1700, with the plethora of smaller producers bringing the 1913 total up to about 16,000 vehicles (King 1989). In 1914, a mechanised belt was added that moved along at a speed of six feet per minute and the process was refined to 45 steps. Ford workers reduced manufacturing time of each car from 12.5 to 1.5 hours, a record-breaking rate. This meant Ford could lower the price and still make a good profit by selling more (Ford 2019). For example, back in 1912 the British built Model Ts were offered for £175 on the domestic market at a time when Austin, a powerful UK based competitor, were offering their smaller slower 10 HP model for £240 (Smith 1968).

Ford's Revolutionary Manufacturing Processes

To keep cars affordable Ford cut every possible cost while still maintaining a safe and fluid environment that would otherwise slow down production. According to Ford:

> In addition to interchangeable parts and the assembly line, there was a sharp division of labour. It was imperative not to waste a second of a worker's time, for that slowed down the belt that needed constant motion to maximize production. Assembly line workers were not responsible for getting their

> own parts, materials, or tools. Another worker did that for them. Ford even reduced the time it took to get extra parts and materials to their proper locations. Instead of runners, intricate modes of slides and trolleys transported whatever was needed. The height of the belt itself was where he thought it would be easiest for workers to stand for extended periods of time. He eliminated time-consuming motions like bending over or reaching up to grab something. He tirelessly analysed the process, micromanaging his plants as if his entire life depended on that day's batch of Model Ts. If a process could be simplified to save a second, Henry Ford ordered the modification. The result was a worker who almost certainly had only one task to do throughout his or her day, and this task likely took little to no training. Ford confronted all possible time wasters and promptly reduced or eliminated them. (Ford 2019)

After the First World War, the Trafford Park plant was extended, and in 1919, 41% of British registered cars were Fords. Unique models were built for the British market and Model T sales quadruple. The Ford Model T stands out as the industry's first global car and by 1921, it accounted for almost 57% of the world's automobile production. In the UK by 1920 26,000 cars were manufactured with all locally manufactured parts. Annual sales rose dramatically from 1485 in 1911 to over 40,000 by 1924. But despite the Ford success there was still reluctance to accept what was right in approach and practices for an American company could be right for a British one (Fig. 5.2).

In 1924 Henry Ford sent over a senior representative to the UK to identify and purchase a suitable site for a larger plant, with access to a deep water port, and a site was acquired at Dagenham [1] although Ford UK production continued to be concentrated at Trafford Park until the Dagenham plant became operational in 1931.

Impact of Trafford Park the Cornerstone of Industrial Parks

Trafford Park was the cornerstone of industrial parks found in the UK, where factory production spread and where first industrial zones were founded. These were set up by multiple production units; the first factories arose somewhat accidentally, however, later on they became interdependently organised that followed ideas of urban and regional planning.

By 1915, 100 American companies had moved into the Trafford Park, peaking at more than 200 by 1933.

Fig. 5.2 1914 image of the factory floor at Ford's Trafford Park plant, in Manchester before the introduction of the moving assembly line which gave British car manufacturers an opportunity to see Ford's new production techniques (Grace's Guide Collection)

Industrial parks provided pools of skilled labour, highly developed ancillary trades and market services, networks of co-operative sub-contracting relationships and rented factory accommodation including power and utilities.

Immense Impact of Trafford Park at Its Peak 1930/1940s Contribution to WW2

At its peak, in the 1930s, the estate boasted the largest private railway system in the UK. According to Herron (2015):

> Nearly 2.5m tonnes of freight was transported through it each year – equating to 3% of all UK freight. Production was almost entirely turned over to war

> materials at the end of that decade, marking Trafford Park as one of the UK's most formidable centres of the Second World War effort. Employment figures for the estate surged, reaching 75,000.

Trafford Park production of war material during the Second World War was immense. It proved to be a good location for producing the Rolls-Royce Merlin engine being close to major transport links and having easy access for the finished product to be supplied to both Metropolitan-Vickers also located in Trafford Park.

According to Scholefield (2004, p. 227):

> Redeveloped by Ford from 1938 under licence, the Rolls-Royce Merlin engines were used to power the Spitfire, Hurricane, Mosquito and the Lancaster aircraft. The 17,316 workers employed in Ford's purpose-built factory had produced 34,000 engines by the war's end. The facility was designed in two separate sections to minimise the impact of bomb damage on production (Nicholls (1996), pp. 103–104). The wood-working factory of F. Hills & Sons built more than 800 Percival Proctor aircraft for the RAF between 1940 and 1945, which were flight tested at the nearby Barton Aerodrome.

Other companies produced gun bearings, steel tracks for Churchill tanks, munitions, Bailey Bridges, and much else. ICI built and operated the first facility in the UK able to produce penicillin in quantity (Nicholls 1996, p. 101).

Conclusion

The Ship Canal project had to be rescued at great expense and was initially a commercial failure (Moulton 1910) although it caused competitive transportation costs to plummet especially with rail. It was built at the beginning of the second industrial revolution but serving the industries and technologies of the first. But more importantly it was a direct catalyst to the creation of the first industrial park (Trafford) in the world (200 factories, 80,000 employees), with its own worker's town.

As in many transformation projects the significant transformation was somewhat later and in a different context, as Trafford Park swept in the second industrial revolution. This had as a great an impact as the first industrial revolution that had a close association with Manchester the first industrial city (Hall 1998). The report of the committee of 1886 had envisioned that along the entire length of the canal great manufacturing establishments would be erected, although this was not within the scope of the project but a consequence of it.

Ford came to Manchester because of the MSC and Trafford Park. Trafford Park through Ford and the adoption of leading manufacturing practices of the second industrial revolution became an economic powerhouse in the UK, and one of the most important industrial centres in WW2.

The significant lesson is not over-looking and recognising emerging opportunities, and then having the mechanisms in the project to address these as they occur. This project occurred in a transition period between two industrial periods with a rapid shift to new emerging technologies. Industrial parks were a new concept that required the right conditions and infrastructure, and the MSC and docks were truly a catalyst for this.

Project Management Lessons

The chapter now analyses the case study and explores a wide range of project management lessons arising from it and the transformative project to draw out lessons of value to contemporary project management. These include:

Defining a Business Case that Goes Beyond the Short to Medium-Term Economic Results

The project ran into financial difficulties before it was completed. Manchester Corporation bailed the project out for the prestige and to avoid losing face (Leech 1907). In reality, the project failed with its business case which did not really grasp the shift from one industrial revolution to another. The project was based on providing a cheaper and more controllable transportation infrastructure. It did not recognise that the coming second industrial revolution would require a different transportation infrastructure and rethink in industrial manufacturing. The project stumbled into this opportunity demonstrating that a business case should go beyond the short to medium-term economic results and incorporate longer term and more broadly defined benefits, having the agility to adjust the business case as new opportunities are presented. It should be an adaptable business case. To do this requires a big picture understanding of an industrial revolution, and the emerging technologies behind it but most importantly how those technologies will enable new applications and capabilities that open new possibilities and opportunities that business can take advantage of. For example, some of the largest companies in the world such as Amazon failed to be profitable for many years. Uber, which now claims to be the world's largest transportation company, still claims that it has never been profitable (Reuters 2018).

The Role of the Project Sponsor
The project sponsor was responsible for steering the project through its phases, and this was a major challenge during the project initiation phase. The political landscape was not favourable with many rivalries and resistance coming from very powerful, wealthy and influential stakeholders like the railway operators, and the City of Liverpool that were directly opposed to the project. The role of the project sponsor was principally to remove these political, legal and financial obstacles.

In contemporary project management and transformation it is important to understand the role of the project sponsor in initiating the project, rallying support, shaping project objectives and direction and removing numerous obstacles including technical, legal, financial, political and military issues.

Recognising That Some Projects Are One-Time Opportunities for Introducing Change
The project investments were substantial. The sponsors recognised that this project was a one-time opportunity for introducing change, like an extensive port facility for cargo handling within close proximity of the manufacturing centre and facilities in and around Manchester, and therefore they needed to prioritise and adequately resource this. In hindsight Trafford Park was the most significant opportunity that arose in the project that was fully realised and had the greatest economic impact over the decades. It also extended the longevity of the canal by increasing its economic life span through new manufacturing trade based on new emerging technologies and manufacturing practices. This opportunity was envisioned () but was not the primary focus of the project.

Contemporary major projects are often one-time opportunities for introducing change. For example, an Enterprise Resource Planning (ERP) project is significant for most organisations as it impacts all the major areas of a business. A retailer with multiple stores, distribution centres and a warehouse, will need to engage multiple business units ranging from finance, retail, operations and supply chain & procurement. These multi-year ERP projects redefine how a business operates and change business processes, bringing industry best practices into the organisation.

Creating Entrepreneurial Partnerships

A wide range of partnerships had to be established that covered all aspects of the project especially where there were known deficits in technology and skills, for example, the technical challenges like a swinging canal. These included partnerships from both the commercial and the public sector with the Manchester Corporation stepping into the project to complete it when it was in serious trouble and private capital was unwilling to take the risk. Post-project entrepreneurial partnerships were the bedrock of Trafford Park providing pools of skilled labour, highly developed ancillary trades and market services. For the Park to provide a sum greater than its parts it required integrated networks of co-operative sub-contracting relationships. This required forward thinking, such as structuring factory site costs over time into a perpetual chief rent system which converted purchase costs into a rental stream, initially set low but rising over 10 years Scott (2001). Eventually, this formula of a giant estate evolved into partnerships with several major US nationals that established a significant presence and grew to 200 plants.

Creating entrepreneurial partnerships and fostering leadership is essential to enabling innovation in contemporary projects and allows them to conquer substantial risks and succeed. This needs both a short and long-term view as the solution evolves and the opportunities crystallise and become tangible. These help to identify the project's short-term capability gaps that require partnerships to fill. Long term these help identify the operation of the solution like the provisioning of extensive on-site services (as Trafford Park Estates did in the case study).

Dealing with Uncertainty

The most complex elements of the project were related to the technical elements. This related to activities like digging the canal, diverting rivers and building seawalls and bridges. One major obstacle was crossing the existing transportation infrastructure of five railways lines and nine main roads, and the Bridgewater Canal had to be carried over the Ship Canal. There were also substantial complicated coordination issues with the workforce spread across eight separate sections, with equipment (173 locomotives, 6300 wagons and trucks) and creation of temporary railway lines.

Contemporary project management presents several types of complexity to consider:

- Structural complexity is a difficulty arising from managing and keeping track of huge numbers of different interconnected tasks and activities.
- Dynamic complexity—(changing relationships among components within a system and between the system and its environment over time) leads to different types of uncertainty.

Managing project complexity deals with uncertainty and requires various strategies including risk reduction.

Assessing and Exploiting Unexpected Opportunities that Are Discovered in the Project

The first opportunity was with the dock facilities and providing magnificent docks, nine in number, with an eye to future needs. The second opportunity was with Trafford Park; this is a perfect example of major unexpected opportunities that came at the tail end of the project. It required a significant investment and the return would take several years to become operational and financially viable as companies had to be attracted, and this required time to set up.

Summary

The MSC provides important lessons for transformation projects in the challenges in initiating a megaproject, rescuing it financially, and then discovering the outcome, in operation, does not meet the expected value and is not economically viable. The megaproject was initiated to serve the needs of a cotton industry manufacturing and production centre born and grounded out of the First Industrial Revolution. Because of opposition it was constructed several decades too late and in competition with, and superseded by, superior railway transportation. However the infrastructure created by the project led to the establishment of Trafford Park, the first industrial estate. This helped to propel Manchester into the Second Industrial Revolution and become a hotbed of new industry and a diversified manufacturing sector driven by emerging technologies and new processes.

References

Carlsson, B. (2004), The Digital Economy: What Is New and What Is Not? *Structural Change and Economic Dynamics* 15: 245–264.

Farnie, D.A. (1980), *The Manchester Ship Canal and the Rise of the Port of Manchester*. Manchester: Manchester University Press.

Ford. (2019), How Henry Ford Revolutionized the Car Industry, Construction Online Journal. Retrieved from http://constructionlitmag.com/culture/how-henry-ford-revolutionized-the-car-industry/.

Hall, P. (1998), The First Industrial City, Manchester, 1760–1830 (Chapter 10). In *Cities in Civilization*. New York, Pantheon Books, pp. 310–347.

Herron, A. (2015), Manchester's Trafford Park, the World's First Industrial Estate—A History of Cities in 50 Buildings, Day 26. *The Guardian*, Wednesday, April 29.

King, P. (1989), *The Motor Men*. London: Quiller Press.

Leech, B. (1907), *History of the Manchester Ship Canal*. Manchester: Sherratt & Hughes.

Maw, P., Wyke, T., and Kidd, A. (2012). Canals, Rivers, and the Industrial City: Manchester's Industrial Waterfront, 1790–1850. *The Economic History Review* 65 (4): 1495–1523. Retrieved from http://www.jstor.org/stable/23271699.

Moulton, H.G. (1910), The Manchester Ship Canal. *Journal of Political Economy*, 18 (6): 449–464.

Nicholls, R. (1996), *Trafford Park: The First Hundred Years*. Cheltenham: Phillimore & Co.

Owen, D. (1983), *The Manchester Ship Canal*. Manchester: Manchester University Press, p. 53.

Reuters. (2018). Retrieved from https://www.reuters.com/article/uber-results/uber-narrows-loss-but-still-a-long-way-from-profitability-idUSL1N1V611I. Accessed February 4, 2019.

Ryall, M.J. (2000), *The Manual of Bridge Engineering*. Thomas Telford, ISBN 978-0-7277-2774-9.

Scholefield, R. (2004), *Manchester's Early Airfields—an extensive article in Moving Manchester*. Lancashire & Cheshire Antiquarian Society.

Smith, M. (1968), Ford of Britain: Yesterday Today…. *Autocar*. 128 (nbr 3766) (April 18): 52–54.

Willan, T. (1977), In W.H. Chaloner and Barrie M. Ratcliffe (Eds.), *Trade and Transport: Essays in Economic History in Honour of T. S. Willan*. Manchester University Press, ISBN 0-8476-6013-3.

No Author

'Trafford Park', n.d. Retrieved February 16, 2019, from http://lamptech.co.uk/Documents/Factory%20-%20UK%20-%20Trafford%20Park.htm.

CHAPTER 6

Conclusions

Abstract From the interpretation of the three historical project case studies projects, the authors using modern terminology, develop twelve significant lessons from their understanding of the key drivers of transformation and project management success. They map these to contemporary digital transformation projects so that contemporary methods and approaches can be enhanced. The authors revisit the challenges of digital transformation and how to adapt project management to meet this challenge. They present a discussion on why project management is more significant than operations management in transformations (digital and business). They conclude with recommendations for the further examination of historical transformation projects in contemporary practice so as to enhance contemporary transformation method and approaches, with priorities and principles for project management.

Keywords Defining lessons · Transformation projects · Key drivers · Contemporary methods and approaches

This book summarises three well known case studies highlighting their relevance to contemporary business and digital transformation and project management. The book concludes by advocating the significance of learning from the examination of historical transformation projects in contemporary practice, by understanding the key drivers of transformation and

M. Kozak-Holland and C. Procter, *Managing Transformation Projects*, https://doi.org/10.1007/978-3-030-33035-4_6

project management success. Significant gains can be made by enhancing contemporary methods and approaches.

Twelve lessons for project management have been developed from the three case studies. These lessons from significant transportation projects from the nineteenth century that are of great relevance to the digital transformation projects of the twenty-first century, namely:

1. Defining a business case that goes beyond the short to medium-term economic results and incorporates longer term and more broadly defined benefits. Having the agility to adjust the business case as new opportunities are presented.
2. Understanding the importance of the project sponsor in initiating the project, rallying support, shaping project objectives and direction and removing numerous obstacles including technical, legal, financial, political and military issues.
3. Recognising that some projects are one-time opportunities for introducing change and therefore need to be prioritised and resourced. This can then create sufficient momentum to deal with inevitable resource shortages later on.
4. Setting up the governance to guide the project teams in their project execution and creating a level of healthy competition between them.
5. Creating entrepreneurial partnerships and fostering leadership to enable innovation in the project and allow it to conquer substantial risks and succeed.
6. Dealing with uncertainty and its relationship to project complexity and managing this through various strategies including risk reduction.
7. Assessing and exploiting unexpected opportunities that are discovered in the project.
8. Creating a culture where project morale is kept up through proactive project communication and by creating a conducive work environment based on the ethical management of a substantial workforce.
9. Using technology innovation in both products and processes to create solutions that can reduce project scope and cost in activities on the critical path.
10. Completing extensive prototyping and piloting to evolve technology solutions.

11. Incorporating agility into projects so as to change course in response to emerging opportunities and threats.
12. Mandating knowledge capture, and transfer between projects, so future projects are part of a continuum.

These are explained in turn:

1. Defining a business case that goes beyond the short- to medium-term economic results, and that incorporates longer term and more broadly defined benefits. Having the agility to adjust the business case as new opportunities are presented.

In all three projects, ensuring the focus was on achieving the business case and, where appropriate, adjusting the business case according to opportunities presented by the project, was more important than following defined processes, managing the project in a business as usual style (as per operations management) and sticking to a plan.

In both the TCR and MSC the business case was critical to the success of the project. The SDR business case was significantly changed to accommodate passengers as well as goods.

The business case for the TCR project was readjusted to incorporate settlers and the creation of towns, and this helped provide a long-term business case based on not just cost savings but economic growth that the towns would generate, and the additional taxes collected. It helped maintain the momentum of the project through a very difficult period.

In the MSC case study the project ran into financial difficulties before it was completed and was bailed out by Manchester Corporation. In reality, the MSC project failed with its business case because it missed the shift from one industrial revolution to another where the canal was not necessarily the cheaper transportation infrastructure. The project stumbled into the opportunity presented by the second industrial revolution and the rethink in industrial manufacturing concentrated on one estate supported by good transportation links.

Both projects were commercial, but the Government acted as a principal stakeholder or sponsor and played a very active role particularly in the TCR. It would have been practically impossible to start the megaproject without this level of public sector support it received since the private sector would not have borne the commercial risk. In contemporary digital transformation projects this risk is more frequently borne by venture capital.

2. Understanding the role of the project sponsor in initiating the project, rallying support, shaping project objectives and direction and removing numerous obstacles including technical, legal, financial, political and military issues.

Pease's role in the SDR project was critical in providing a vision, understanding the political landscape and constraints and being flexible to new ideas. His industry experience as a businessman and entrepreneur was crucial in putting together a consortium to drive the project and secure the necessary funding. Stephenson persuaded Pease to change direction on the approach and technology, who was flexible enough to quickly recognise the new opportunity presented by the project. Later Pease stepped in at critical points in the project where it potentially could get into trouble and took actions to mitigate the risk.

Lincoln's role was absolutely pivotal in initiating the TCR project. By understanding the political landscape, he kept the project alive in the most challenging of times and his industry experience as a railroad lawyer was invaluable.

With the MSC project, the sponsor had a major challenge during the project initiation phase. The political landscape was not favourable with many rivalries and resistance coming from very powerful, wealthy and influential stakeholders. The role of the project sponsor in removing political, legal and financial obstacles was vital to ensuring that the project progressed.

In all three case studies the project sponsor characteristics were similar in having many business connections to bring partners to the table, good industry experience related to the areas affected by the project, ability to provide a guiding project vision, and being politically aware of how to deal with the surrounding groups and players who could negatively impact the project because of their own competing agendas.

3. Recognising that some projects are one-time opportunities for introducing change and therefore need to be prioritised and resourced. This can then create sufficient momentum to deal with inevitable resource shortages later on.

All three projects were one-time opportunities because of the constellation of political will, funding and timing, which would not be repeated. Thus, for example in the TCR case study the astronomical costs and the lack of political opposition because of the civil war made this a one-time opportunity which Lincoln took advantage of and initiated the project. The wire-telegraph, intertwined with the operation of the railroad, was a further one-time opportunity.

In all three cases sunk costs mid-project made it financially impractical to back out of the project so they had to continue until completion. This issue is characteristic of many contemporary megaprojects. Indeed Flyvbjerg argues that both cost and time are deliberately underestimated in megaprojects in order to create unstoppable projects (Flyvbjerg 2014).

In the MSC case study, the mega project was a one-time opportunity for introducing change, the extensive port facility for cargo handling very close to the manufacturing centre. Trafford Park was the most significant opportunity that extended the longevity of the canal, increasing its economic life span through new manufacturing trade based on emerging technologies and manufacturing practices.

4. Setting up the governance to guide the project teams in their project execution and creating a level of healthy competition between them.

In all three projects new legislation was required to allow the transformative projects to be undertaken. In the face of opposition, the sponsor had to ensure that legislation became an enabler rather than a fetter to the projects. For example, in the TCR project, the Government Acts controlled governance to direct the stakeholders, particularly the railroad companies. The same lessons apply to contemporary transformations; the governance drives the project and behaviour of the stakeholders.

In contemporary project management and transformation, governance is critical to success but needs to be set up at multiple levels starting at a programme level and then within projects. The governance must be able to respond quickly to risk and issue escalations, resolve competing priorities, have the authority to make decisions, make those decisions promptly and monitor programme/project performance. This may be coordinated through a Project Management Office (PMO) that can provide programme and project oversights. The PMO should be attached to the executive office and so to the strategic and tactical business objectives with representation from business and technology and strong relationships to strategic planners, business unit leaders, and the enterprise architecture office, enterprise service owners and vendors. The PMO should be in place over the project duration to deliver the expected outcomes in the expected time frame.

5. Creating entrepreneurial partnerships and fostering leadership to enable innovation in the project and allow it to conquer substantial risks and succeed.

Pease encouraged Stephenson to open up a factory and set up entrepreneurial partnerships to drive the project benefit, by solving technical problems and lowering the risk. This factory later became part of the long-term vision and operation management, producing next generation locomotives. According to Carlsson (2004):

> Schumpeter (1911) argued that economic growth is a result of innovations, i.e., new combinations of products, processes, markets, sources of supply, and organizations. The number of potential innovations (i.e., the opportunity set or state space) is virtually unlimited. This means that at any moment only a small subset of all technical possibilities has been identified and only a yet smaller subset has been exploited commercially. New combinations are discovered through experimentation. In order to identify more technical possibilities, more attempts (experiments) are necessary.

Lincoln's experience in the Civil War and recognition of Haupt's role with the Corps gave him insight into the TCR project on how to innovate to solve the most critical problems. Entrepreneurial partnerships were set up with the 2 commercial railroad companies, and the Chinese government who met the workforce gap in the project.

In the MSC project a wide range of partnerships were established covering technical, legal and financial aspects of the project where there were known deficits. These included commercial entities and the public sector in Manchester Corporation who stepped into the project to complete it when it was in serious trouble. Post-project entrepreneurial partnerships formed Trafford Park and provided pools of skilled labour, highly developed ancillary trades and market services. Eventually, this giant estate evolved into partnerships with several major US companies and grew to 200 plants.

In all 3 case studies entrepreneurial partnerships themselves tapped into a broader range of resources and skills which provided the projects greater leverage. Fostering leadership for innovation is initiated by senior leaders who need to create a conducive environment to help encourage this.

6. Dealing with uncertainty and its relationship to project complexity and managing this through various strategies including risk reduction.

In the TCR complexities lay with the range of stakeholders and keeping the workforce working at full capacity. The total number of stakeholders and groups was high, and they had varied expectations and agendas. To keep the workforce fully occupied required a constant supply of materials, equipment and supplies, and this required an 18,000 mile supply chain (30 ships).

In the MSC the technical elements of the project were the most complex like digging the canal, diverting rivers and building seawalls and bridges, and crossing the existing transportation infrastructure of five railways lines and nine main roads, and a canal. There was also the coordination of the workforce and the substantial equipment (173 locomotives, 6300 wagons and trucks) across the eight separate sections.

In both the TCR and MSC projects, managing the risk created by this technical complexity involving multiple stakeholders was fundamental to reducing the uncertainty of the projects achieving their objectives.

7. (Related to 1 above) Assessing and exploiting unexpected opportunities that are discovered in the project.

Pease and Stephenson assessed and exploited unexpected opportunities that were discovered in the SDR project and changed transportation solutions. The decisions were significant and risky with changes in technology requiring much innovation.

In the MSC the first opportunity was with the dock facilities with an eye to future needs. The second opportunity was with the Trafford Park industrial estate which was unexpected and required a significant investment, with a protracted return.

In both the SDR and MSC projects unexpected opportunities were discovered in different phases. This had an impact on how these were leveraged by the teams. SDR was able to better to react to changes in technology and switched to locomotives. Whereas with the MSC the industrial park arrived at the tail end of the project.

8. Creating a culture where project morale is kept up through proactive project communication and by creating a conducive work environment based on the ethical management of a substantial workforce.

This was especially notable in the TCR project. According to Kraus (1969) a large Chinese workforce of 10,000 was drafted to quickly fill the labour gaps by the CPRR, attracted by relatively high rates of pay. The workforce was well organised with provision for the health, safety and welfare of the workers.

It has been well established in practice and in the literature since work around the Hawthorne effect (Mayo 1945) that a well-cared for workforce is more productive. Creating a culture with a positive project morale starts with assessing organisational receptiveness and readiness, and an impact assessment of the changes associated with the project/transformation. This then leads to identifying and deploying various strategies to help groups and individuals address the changes. This is kept up through the transformation by proactive communications and by creating a conducive work environment based on the ethical management of a substantial workforce.

9. Using technology innovation in both products and processes to create solutions that can reduce project scope and cost in activities on the critical path.

In the SDR project the technology was under-developed, untried and untested and the locomotive factory provided a conducive environment to evolve the engines to double or triple the best current speeds. This allowed for a decision to stay the course with this improved locomotive technology over stationary steam cable engines.

Haupt's Civil War experience and understanding of the critical role that railroads played gave him insights into the innovation required to solve the most critical problems in the TCR project. By evolving new technology (swivel wheel trucks) and processes, solutions were created to solve the problem of gradients which greatly reduced project scope and cost.

10. Completing extensive prototyping and piloting to evolve technology solutions.

Project management is not conducive to innovation as the focus is on results and delivery. The 3 case studies demonstrate how projects effectively incorporated innovation.

In the SDR case study extensive prototyping and piloting was required to evolve and adapt various new emerging technologies for all systems from rail tracks, to propulsion and traction systems. These all required extensive development work, and then integration into a holistic transportation solution.

In the TCR case study Herman Haupt's Construction Corps completed extensive prototyping and piloting to evolve and adapt various new emerging technologies for transportation solutions. For example, they mastered rapid bridge reconstruction and made this operational through experimentation and laboratory tests. They came up with new designs for bridges, which was significant with over 2000 bridges required, and the principal constraint to getting materials to site.

Both case studies demonstrate that projects need to be exploratory to make discoveries, as not all is revealed up front in the pre-project assessment. A wide range of complex challenges and issues only come to light during the project that require a degree of exploration and discovery to come up with ideas and the best solution. For example, challenges and issues related to emerging technology, or the integration of multiple technologies, and evolving these into a working solution will meet the operational service levels. Other challenges and issues that are typically far more difficult to solve relate to organisations, stakeholders and people.

11. (Also related to 1 and 7 above) Incorporating agility into projects so as to change course in response to emerging opportunities and threats.

All three projects took a number of substantial changes in direction as transportation alternatives were evaluated for their pay-back (project and long term), feasibility, ability to complete and risk. This flexibility required a relatively high level of agility to accommodate a high degree of uncertainty.

Being nimble and quick can be crucial to the overall success for several reasons. Rapid changes in technology over short periods have to be accommodated in a project. Technology enables new applications and capabilities that open new business opportunities that could not be anticipated at the planning stage.

An agile project recognises and welcomes the change that technology will have on the project. Technology roadmaps are identified, using techniques like technology landscape mapping which plot the maturity of a technology in its evolution over the course of time. Recognition of the inevitability of change was fundamental to the evolution of Agile in the late twentieth century: Responding to change over following a plan was a key component of the original Agile manifesto. While Agile originated in software development and is of great significance to contemporary IT projects (Jørgensen 2018; Dingsoyr et al. 2012), it has great relevance to all project management (Serrador and Pinto 2015; Lensges et al. 2018). Agility of course can increase risk and thus learning from the effective adoption of an agile approach from an historical project can provide important lessons for contemporary projects.

12. Mandating knowledge capture, and transfer between projects, so future projects are part of a continuum.

The SDR project team, under Stephenson, had to increase their fundamental knowledge in core technologies. For Stephenson this was critical for the project and the future of railways. Stephenson recruited Timothy Hackworth, one of the engineers from the Puffing Billy project and national expert. He also employed skilled mechanics who could quickly put ideas into practical use and innovate the manufacturing processes for the locomotive.

Mandating knowledge capture, and transfer between projects is essential, so future projects are part of a continuum, especially where the technology is similar and evolving quickly. This becomes a challenge where multiple projects start up simultaneously. The PMO has an important role to play in establishing in the organisation smooth knowledge transfer, and also in forming enterprise views of architectures (business, solution, technical). This is akin to planning the infrastructure within a city environment.

The Key Drivers of Project Management and Transformation Success

From the list of common lessons from the case studies the key drivers that need to be addressed are:

- How to establish a clear vision and a journey roadmap?
- How to introduce innovation and adopt it within the project so that it does not create uncertainty and increase costs, and then use it for both technology and processes?
- How to establish new emerging business models?
- How to manage organisational resistance to change?

Lessons for the Contemporary Business World

The 3 case studies demonstrate how recent theoretical work allows for a richer discussion than the limitations of process and technique in existing bodies of project management knowledge. In this development of theory, project management can learn from more established disciplines including history and organisational theory.

In his important book *Reconstructing Project Management* (2013), summarised in a paper later that year (2013), Morris argues:

> …in the early 1970s … the discipline [project management], as it had now clearly become, began to be seriously affected by social, economic, political, and environmental issues… The theory-light engineering project management available at this time was just not rich or powerful enough to help managers deal with the uncertainties created by this new generation of externalities.

He suggests that the adoption of multiple perspectives and reference to research from other disciplines can greatly strengthen project management research and practice. This is supported by other project management researchers. For example, Cicmil and Hodgson (2006) presented the case for more critical project case studies that reflect the political, social and ethical dimensions of project management work. Additionally Morris (2013) emphasised the economic and environmental issues that characterise megaprojects. Morris argues that this approach allows for a much richer analysis, providing more depth than the traditional triple constraint of time, cost and scope. It also conceptually supports the argument of decontextualisation of project management lessons into sets of best practices.

Why Project Management Is More Significant Than Operations Management in Transformation

From the three case studies key characteristics of transformation include the unknowable, exploratory, reflexivity and improvisation, collaboration and agility.

The transformation journey is into the unknown and it can be a road trip without a destination. The route or the goal is underdetermined, inchoate or ill-defined and sometimes all three (Scranton 2010). This is in contrast to a predictable journey with an expected destination. Tiersky (*CIO* 2017) argues that in digital transformation projects this requires developing a clear vision of how an organisation will meet their customers' future digital needs.

Transformation requires exploration and discovery that involves uncertainty, complexity and management, without an anticipated return to investors. This is in contrast to routinised operations and projects which are standardised, repetitive and unimaginative.

By definition, disruptive projects require agility to find the best path, which implies welcoming stumbles and failure as part of exploration, and then reflecting on what has happened. This in turn involves improvisation or innovation of emerging technologies and processes. This requires collaboration outside of the organisational boundaries, finding sources of expertise to interact with to find solutions. The project charter itself needs to be set up in such a way as to be conducive to innovation.

Digital Transformation requires agility to respond to the situation at hand. A transformation is a major undertaking for most non-digital organisations and can take a year or two to complete; a lack of agility can in fact create substantial delays where the original planned solution is delivered but clearly does not lead to progress.

Author Recommendations—Enhancing Contemporary Transformation Method and Approaches

The authors strongly recommend project management should be taking a leading role in digital transformation because it provides the overall framework for all the elements of a transformation. They also recommend adjusting methods and approaches by introducing the following into the project management Bodies of Knowledge (BOKs):

1. the missing dimensions of project management (the political, social, ethical, economic and environmental),
2. both contemporary and historical case studies from megaprojects and transformations (with a level of decontextualisation),
3. adjusted project management priorities and principles:
    a. less dominated by the operations paradigm,
    b. less prescriptive and technical (traditional triple constraint of time, cost and scope),
    c. less focused on the process model of project management and more focused on partnerships with stakeholders,
    d. less focused on short-term results and delivery and
    e. more focused on long-term changes,
    f. more exploration, unique endeavours, opportunities (one time), the unknowable and discovery of the unknown (versus the known),
    g. more reflexivity, improvisation and agility,
    h. setting the project up so that it welcomes and enables innovation.

Gartner's advocacy of introducing the approach of product portfolio management in an organisation could be used in transforming less strategic applications, of which there are typically between 200 and 1000, which would not be run as projects. This would reduce the volume of smaller projects (Scott et al. 2018) and concentrate project resources on the transformation of the more strategic applications (up to 200).

This approach will help equip managers well for disruptive or transformational projects. Transformation projects are critical to an organisation in the return on investment, realignment of strategy, introduction of new business models, preparation for the digital business world and becoming more resilient to competition.

Summary

In reviewing the 3 case studies there is strong evidence of the relevance of historical project lessons to contemporary business practice, and support of transformations. Most notably in the areas of vision and leadership and how sponsors and engineers guided the transformation projects of the past. The skills are clearly pertinent today.

The analysis of historical case studies and their interpretation using modern terminology, can enrich our understanding of transformation and project management success and failure, and empower international scholars, and learning for the future.

Final Thoughts

The analysis of the three case studies demonstrates that transformation and project management is not a new discipline. It suggests that the core knowledge areas of project management, as defined today, were used extensively in great historical projects. What further work is needed? The publication very much supports further research into historical projects and the process of building up knowledge of historical projects and lessons management and expanding the general body of project management knowledge (see Appendix). With globalisation it is important to address the different cultural aspects of project management. Thus countries around the world can have their own examples of historical projects within their own culture to refer to and not be presented with just a western view of twentieth-century project management they may not readily identify with. They need to determine which historical case studies to use and which to exclude.

For future work what would further Historical Case Studies look like? Based on the selection criteria periods of rapid change should be examined. For example, further research into the 3 industrial revolutions of the last 250 years.

How to Draw Lessons from Historical Case Studies

The following reviews the methodology, research methods and techniques as to how to draw lessons from historical case studies. The learning from the examination of Historical Transformation Projects better prepares practitioners understanding for the future.

Historiography

Historiography is the study of the writing of history, of historical perspectives over time, the changing research interests of historians and a methodology of historical research and presentation. For example, the views on Ancient Egypt changed between 1900 and 2000, as the research interests of Egyptologists changed from finding treasures, to discovering habitats and skeletal remains. Historiography examines the changing interpretations of historical events in the works of individual historians.

Traditionally historians have taken a narrative-based approach. Stone (1979) defined a narrative as being organised chronologically, focused on a single coherent story, descriptive rather than analytical, concerned with people not abstract circumstances, and dealing with the particular and specific, rather than the collective and statistical. He reported that:

> More and more of the 'new historians' are now trying to discover what was going on inside people's heads in the past, and what it was like to live in the past, questions which inevitably lead back to the use of narrative. (Stone 1979, p. 13)

The past is increasingly seen as a narrative which is constructed through historical writing. Historical facts only become useful when assembled with other historical evidence, and the process of assembling this evidence is understood as a particular historiographical approach.

The *Journal of Management History* has cultivated the use of historiography in management research. In a special edition in 2008 (Grattan 2008) it gathered general advice from eminent historians and suggested a particular approach for the management historian:

> The aim is to encourage the writing of management histories that can contribute to our knowledge of the past but also can form the basis for further hypotheses and insights in the field of management. (Grattan 2008, p. 174)

Historians need to be empathetic to a period and handle the facts in-line with the society and ideas that existed at the time. Grattan (2008, p. 176) discusses the use of general historiography and its particular application to management history stating that historiography is essentially an art or a craft.

> This brief consideration of the nature of history is consistent with the idea that the events of the past can be crafted into a meaningful account, rather

> than attempting to treat the evidence scientifically. The raw material, the clay, of history is evidence and empathy with this material is essential in the writing of history.

This advice can be equally applied to project management.

Approach to the Three Case Studies

The methodology used in this book was pluralist. Using an interpretive approach, a combination of case study and historiographical research was used with an emphasis on examining narratives. A supportive methodology, interdisciplinarity, was used to guide the research. The three steps of historiography were followed:

- Investigation, including data collection methods like literature reviews, interviews and oral histories, field research and on-site visits.
- Synthesis, including content analysis, constant comparison method, thematic analysis and analysis of narratives.
- Interpretation, including the theoretical framework, cross checking and testing for coherence, extraction, transfer and transformation of historical lessons into contemporary lessons.

A summary of the research methods used are outlined in Fig. 6.1.

The simple description of the methods and techniques of research provided in this book can be adapted by students of project management to develop their own historical case studies of direct relevance to their own contexts and societies and be of significant value to contemporary project management. They can contribute significantly to closing the gap between project management theory and practice and expand our knowledge base beyond prescriptive bodies of knowledge.

Author's Thesis Reference

In 2014 Mark Kozak-Holland published his Ph.D./Ph.D. thesis:

The Relevance of Historical Project Lessons to Contemporary Business Practice Found on:

http://usir.salford.ac.uk/30644/1/Thesis_Relevance_of_Historical_Project_Lessons_v_4_3.pdf

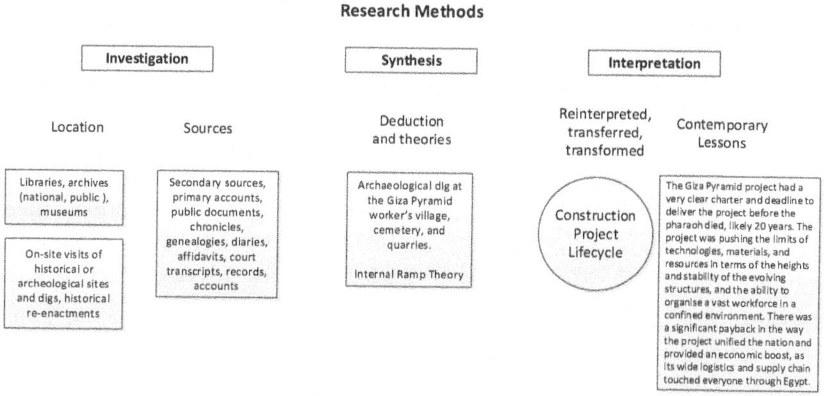

Fig. 6.1 Research methods expanded with specific examples (Kozak-Holland 2014) taken from the Giza Pyramid case study

Thesis Description

Despite worldwide growth in project management there is a significant gap between research and practice. The discipline lacks a unified theory and established body of research. Bodies of knowledge reflect process and technique yet frequently neglect the political, social, ethical, economic and environmental dimensions of project management.

The theory of established academic disciplines evolves through history and by a study of their historical antecedents. The principal question of this thesis thus is concerned with the relevance of historical projects lessons to contemporary business practice and contemporary project management? The secondary question is concerned with the development of an approach to studying this. In addressing these questions the thesis examines some of the challenges with contemporary project management literature, and literature that discusses the relevance of historical project lessons including that from other disciplines such as management.

The thesis describes the use of a qualitative approach, based upon an interpretivist epistemology as the basis for use of case studies. In addition it discusses the use of historiography and interdisciplinarity. It then examines the methods used and findings of nine publications and their contributions to the research questions.

The findings of the thesis establish that project management has a deep history and has been successfully used by developing cultures since the beginnings of civilisation. They also establish that historical projects, when interpreted through a business/project management lens, can be understood by contemporary project managers and are of significant and meaningful value to contemporary business practice. The methodology to establish this is also described. Thus the thesis will contribute to both the project management body of knowledge, by broadening it out and augmenting contemporary case studies, and to addressing the theory–practice gaps within project management.

References

Carlsson, B. (2004), The Digital Economy: What Is New and What Is Not? *Structural Change and Economic Dynamics* 15: 245–264.

Cicmil, S., and Hodgson, D. (2006), *Making Projects Critical: An Introduction.* In Hodgson, D., Cummings, S., and Bridgman, T. (2011), The Relevant Past: Why the History of Management Should Be Critical for Our Future. *Academy of Management Learning & Education* 10 (1): 77–93.

Dingsoyr, T., Nerur, S., Balijepally, V., and Moe, N. B. (2012), A decade of agile methodologies: Towards explaining agile software development. *Journal of Systems and Software* 85: 1213–1221. https://doi.org/10.1016/j.jss.2012.02.033.

Flyvbjerg, B. (2014), What You Should Know About Megaprojects and Why: An Overview. *Project Management Journal* 45 (2): 6–19.

Grattan, R. (2008), Crafting Management History. *Journal of Management History* 14 (2): 174–183.

Jørgensen, M. (2018), Do Agile Methods Work for Large Software Projects? https://doi.org/10.1007/978-3-319-91602-6_12, *Agile Processes in Software Engineering and Extreme Programming*, 19th International Conference, XP 2018, Porto, Portugal, May 21–25, 2018, Proceedings.

Kozak-Holland, M. (2014), PhD/PhD Thesis of Mark Kozak-Holland. Retrieved from http://usir.salford.ac.uk/30644/1/Thesis_Relevance_of_Historical_Project_Lessons_v_4_3.pdf.

Kraus, G. (1969), Chinese Laborers and the Construction of the Central Pacific. *Utah Historical Quarterly* 37 (1) (Winter): 41–57. PDF Copyright Utah State Historical Society, used by permission. Retrieved January 21, 2019, from http://cprr.org/Museum/Chinese_Laborers.html.

Lensges, M., Kloppenborg, T. J., and Forte, F. (2018), Identifying key Agile behaviors that enhance traditional project management methodology. *Journal of Strategic Innovation and Sustainability* 13 (2): 22–36.

Mayo, E. (1945), *Social Problems of an Industrial Civilization*. Boston: Division of Research, Graduate School of Business Administration, Harvard University, p. 72.

Morris, P. (2013), Reconstructing Project Management (Wiley). Summarized latest book in an article for *Project Management Journal* 44 (5): 6–23.

Serrador, P., and Pinto, J. (2015), Does Agile work?—A quantitative analysis of agile project success. *International Journal of Project Management* 33. https://doi.org/10.1016/j.ijproman.2015.01.006

Scranton, P. (2010), *Projects as Business History: Surveying the Landscape*. New Brunswick, NJ: Rutgers University Press.

Stone, L. (1979), The Revival Of Narrative: Reflections On A New Old History. *Past and Present* 85 (Nov 1979): 3–24, quote on p. 13. https://www.jstor.org/stable/650677?seq=1#page_scan_tab_contents.

Tiersky, H. (2017), Navigating Digital Transformation. *CIO Magazine*. Retrieved from https://www.cio.com/article/3179607/e-commerce/5-top-challenges-to-digital-transformation-in-the-enterprise.html.

Gartner

Scott, D., Mingay, S., and Hotle, M. (2018), Leveraging Digital Product Management: A Gartner Trend Insight Report, Gartner; Published: November 16, 2018 ID: G00373974; Analyst(s): Donna Scott, Simon Mingay, and Matthew Hotle.

Glossary

The First Industrial Revolution began in the UK about 1760 (Wrigley 2018) and was the transition to new manufacturing processes in textiles through the use of steam power, the development of machine tools and the rise of the factory system.

The Second Industrial Revolution began to occur in the United States after 1870, with the end of the US Civil War, American entrepreneurs were building on the advancements made in Britain with new forms of transportation, the emergence of electricity and innovations in industry that included new steel making processes (Morison 1966), and gradually grew to include chemicals, petroleum (refining and distribution) and the automotive industry.

The Third Industrial Revolution or the digital revolution is the shift from mechanical and analogue electronic technology to digital electronics which began anywhere from the late 1950s to the late 1970s.

M. Kozak-Holland and C. Procter, *Managing Transformation Projects*, https://doi.org/10.1007/978-3-030-33035-4

Literature References

Adidas miCoach Smart Ball Project. (2014). Retrieved February 16, 2019, from https://www.semiconductorstore.com/press/2014/adidas-miCoach-Smart-Ball/769.

Agricola, G. (1913), *De re Metallica*, trans. Hoover. New York: Dover, p. 156.

Allen, Cecil J. (1974 [1964]), *The North Eastern Railway*. Shepperton: Ian Allan.

Ambrose, Stephen E. (2001), *Nothing Like It in the World: The Men Who Built the Transcontinental Railroad, 1863–1869*. New York: Simon & Schuster.

Ashton, T. (1948), *The Industrial Revolution 1760–1830*. Oxford: Oxford University Press, p. 71.

Baccarini, D. (1996), The concept of project complexity—A review. *International Journal of Project Management* 14: 201–204. https://doi.org/10.1016/0263-7863(95)00093-3.

Bailey, W. (1908), The Story of the Central Pacific. Retrieved from http://cprr.org/Museum/Bailey_CPRR_1908.html.

Bain, D.H. (2000), Pride and Pitfalls Along a Coast to Coast Track, by Michael Kenney. *Boston Globe*, January 10. A book review: Empire Express: Building the First Transcontinental Railroad.

Barras, R. (2009), *Building Cycles: Growth and Instability*. Chichester: Wiley.

Boutinet, J. (2004), *Anthropologie Du Projet* [Anthropology of the Project]. Paris: PUF.

Brady, T., Davies, A., and Nightingale, P. (2012), Dealing with Uncertainty in Complex Projects: Revisiting Klein and Meckling. *International Journal of Managing Projects in Business* 15 (4): 718–736.

Bredillet, C. (2010), Blowing Hot and Cold on Project Management. *Project Management Journal* 41 (3): 4–20.

M. Kozak-Holland and C. Procter, *Managing Transformation Projects*, https://doi.org/10.1007/978-3-030-33035-4

Brunninge, O. (2009), Using History in Organisations: How Managers Make Purposeful Reference to History in Strategy Processes. *Journal of Organisational Change Management* 22 (1): 8–26.

Buffa. (1984), *Meeting the Competitive Challenge.* Irwin, IL.

Burke, J. (1985), *Connections.* New York: Simon & Schuster.

Cameron, B. (2015), CIOs' Top Five Career-Ending Digital Transformation Challenges. Forrester.

Carlos, Ann M., and Lewis, Frank D. (1995), The Creative Financing of an Unprofitable Enterprise: The Grand Trunk Railway of Canada, 1853–1881. *Explorations in Economic History* 32 (3): 273–301.

Carlsson, B. (2004), The Digital Economy: What Is New and What Is Not? *Structural Change and Economic Dynamics* 15: 245–264.

Cepeda, G., and Martin, D. (2005), A Review of Case Studies Publishing in Management Decision 2003–2004: Guides and Criteria for Achieving Quality in Qualitative Research. *Management Decision* 43 (6): 851–876.

Challis, David Milbank, and Rush, Andy. (2009), The Railways of Britain: An Unstudied Map Corpus. *Imago Mundi* 61 (2): 186–214. https://doi.org/10.1080/03085690902923614.

Chapman, R. (2016), A Framework for Examining the Dimensions and Characteristics of Complexity Inherent Within Rail Megaprojects. *International Journal of Project Management* 34: 937–956.

Cicmil, S., and Hodgson, D. (2006), *Making Projects Critical: An Introduction.* In Hodgson, D., Cummings, S., and Bridgman, T. (2011), The Relevant Past: Why the History of Management Should Be Critical for Our Future. *Academy of Management Learning & Education* 10 (1): 77–93.

Cicmil, S., Williams, T., Thomas, J., and Hodgson, D. (2006), Rethinking Project Management: Researching the Actuality of Projects. *International Journal of Project Management* 24: 675–686.

Clark, R. (1985), *Works of Man: History of Invention and Engineering, from the Pyramids to the Space Shuttle* (1st American Edition, 8 × 10 Hard cover ed.). New York: Viking Penguin, p. 352 (indexed).

Davies, A., MacAulay, S., DeBarro, T., and Thurston M. (2014), Making Innovation Happen in a Megaproject: London's Crossrail Suburban Railway System. *Project Management Journal* 45 (6): 25–37.

Dimitriou, H., Ward, E.J., and Wright, P.G. (2015), *Lessons for Mega Transport Project Developments and the Future of UK Cities and Regions.* Retrieved from https://assets.publishing.service.gov.uk/government/uploads/system/uploads/attachment_data/file/499051/future-of-cities-mega-transport-projects.pdf.

Dingsoyr, T., Nerur, S., Balijepally, V., and Moe, N.B. (2012), A Decade of Agile Methodologies: Towards Explaining Agile Software Development. *Journal of*

Systems and Software 85: 1213–1221. https://doi.org/10.1016/j.jss.2012.02.033.

Farnie, D.A. (1980), *The Manchester Ship Canal and the Rise of the Port of Manchester*. Manchester: Manchester University Press.

Flyvbjerg, B. (2006), Five Misunderstandings About Case-Study Research. *Qualitative Inquiry* 12 (2): 219–245.

Flyvbjerg, B. (2014), What You Should Know About Megaprojects and Why: An Overview. *Project Management Journal* 45 (2): 6–19.

Forbes. (2016), Why 84% of Companies Fail at Digital Transformation. Retrieved from https://www.forbes.com/sites/brucerogers/2016/01/07/why-84-of-companies-fail-at-digital-transformation/#5f1b943397bd.

Ford. (2019), How Henry Ford Revolutionized the Car Industry, Construction Online Journal. Retrieved from http://constructionlitmag.com/culture/how-henry-ford-revolutionized-the-car-industry/.

Ford Motor Company. (2019), Company Timeline. Retrieved from https://corporate.ford.com/history.html.

Gaddis, J. (2002), *The Landscape of History: How Historians Map the Past*. New York: Oxford University Press.

Garel, G. (2012), A History of Project Management Models. *International Journal of Project Management* 21 (2013): 663–669.

Gauthier, J., and Ika, L. (2013), Foundations of Project Management Research: An Explicit and Six-Facet Ontological Framework. *Project Management Journal* 43 (5): 5–23.

Geraldi, J., and Söderlund, J. (2012), Classics in Project Management: Revisiting the Past, Creating the Future. *International Journal of Managing Projects in Business* 5 (4): 559–577.

Gopalakrishnan, B. (2013), Project Managing Global Business Transformation Projects: Tips and Tricks. Paper presented at PMI® Global Congress 2013—North America, New Orleans, LA. Newtown Square, PA: Project Management Institute.

Grattan, R. (2008), Crafting Management History. *Journal of Management History* 14 (2): 174–183.

Hall, P. (1998), The First Industrial City, Manchester, 1760–1830 (Chapter 10). In *Cities in Civilization*. New York, Pantheon Books, pp. 310–347.

Hammer, M., and Champy, J. (1993), *Reengineering the Corporation: A Manifesto for Business Revolution*. New York: Harper Collins.

Heath, E. (1928), A Railroad Record That Defies Defeat: How Central Pacific Laid Ten Miles of Track in One Day Back in 1869. *Southern Pacific Bulletin* XVI (5): 3–5. Retrieved February 15, 2019, from http://cprr.org/Museum/Southern_Pacific_Bulletin/Ten_Mile_Day.html.

Herron, A. (2015), Manchester's Trafford Park, the World's First Industrial Estate—A History of Cities in 50 Buildings, Day 26. *The Guardian*, Wednesday, April 29.

Hill, T. (1881), The painting depicts the ceremony of the driving of the *Last Spike* at Promontory Summit, UT, on May 10, 1869, joining the rails of the Central Pacific Railroad and the Union Pacific Railroad.

Hoole, K. (1974a), *A Regional History of the Railways of Great Britain: Volume IV the North East.* Exeter: David & Charles.

Hoole, K. (1974b), *Stockton and Darlington Railway: Anniversary Celebrations of the World's First Steam Worked Public Railway.* North Yorkshire: Dalesman.

Hudson, J. (1982), Towns of the Western Railroads. *Great Plains Quarterly* 2 (Winter): 41–54.

Hutchison, C. (2015), *A History of American Civil War Literature.* Cambridge: Cambridge University Press.

Galloway, C.E., John Debo. (1950), *The First Transcontinental Railroad.* New York: Simmons-Boardman, Ch. 7.

Jørgensen, M. (2018), Do Agile Methods Work for Large Software Projects? https://doi.org/10.1007/978-3-319-91602-6_12, *Agile Processes in Software Engineering and Extreme Programming*, 19th International Conference, XP 2018, Porto, Portugal, May 21–25, 2018, Proceedings.

Kieser, A. (1994), Why Organisation Theory Needs Historical Analyses—And How This Should Be Performed. *Organisation Science* 5 (4): 608–620.

King, P. (1989), *The Motor Men.* London: Quiller Press.

King, G. (2012), Where the Buffalo No Longer Roamed. Retrieved February 15, 2019, from https://www.smithsonianmag.com/history/where-the-buffalo-no-longer-roamed-3067904/.

Kirby, M. (2002), *The Origins of Railway Enterprise: The Stockton and Darlington Railway 1821–1863.* Cambridge: Cambridge University Press.

Klein, M. (1987), Book Union Pacific: The Birth of a Railroad 1862–1893. University of Minnesota Press, pp. 100–101. KPMG's Global Transformation Study (2016), Succeeding in disruptive times. Retrieved from https://assets.kpmg.com/content/dam/kpmg/pdf/2016/05/global-transformation-study-2016.pdf.

Klein, M. (2006), Union Pacific: Volume I, 1862–1893 and Financing the Transcontinental Railroad. The Gilder Lehrman, Institute of American History. Retrieved from https://www.gilderlehrman.org/history-by-era/development-west/essays/financing-transcontinental-railroad.

Kozak-Holland, M. (2014), PhD/PhD Thesis of Mark Kozak-Holland. Retrieved from http://usir.salford.ac.uk/30644/1/Thesis_Relevance_of_Historical_Project_Lessons_v_4_3.pdf.

Kraus, G. (1969), Chinese Laborers and the Construction of the Central Pacific. *Utah Historical Quarterly* 37 (1) (Winter): 41–57. PDF Copyright Utah State

Historical Society, used by permission. Retrieved January 21, 2019, from http://cprr.org/Museum/Chinese_Laborers.html.

Kwak, Y., and Chih, Y. (2009), Towards a Comprehensive Understanding of Public Private Partnerships for Infrastructure Development. *California Management Review* 51 (2): 51–78.

Lamond, D. (2006), Management and Its History: The Worthy Endeavour of the Scribe. *Journal of Management History* 12 (1): 5–11.

Lamond, D. (2008), Management History in Other Places. *Journal of Management History* 14 (2): 184–193.

Launius, R. (1965), The Railroads and the Space Program Revisited: Historical Analogues and the Stimulation of Commercial Space Operations. *Astropolitics* 12 (2–3): 167–179.

Leech, B. (1907), *History of the Manchester Ship Canal.* Manchester: Sherratt & Hughes.

Lensges, M., Kloppenborg, T.J., and Forte, F. (2018), Identifying Key Agile Behaviors that Enhance Traditional Project Management Methodology. *Journal of Strategic Innovation and Sustainability* 13 (2): 22–36.

Lundin, R., and Soderholm, A. (1995), A Theory of the Temporary Organisation. *Scandinavian Journal of Management* 11: 437–455 (quotes from 438).

Maw, P., Wyke, T., and Kidd, A. (2012), Canals, Rivers, and the Industrial City: Manchester's Industrial Waterfront, 1790–1850. *The Economic History Review* 65 (4): 1495–1523. Retrieved from http://www.jstor.org/stable/23271699.

Mayo, E. (1945), *Social Problems of an Industrial Civilization.* Boston: Division of Research, Graduate School of Business Administration, Harvard University, p. 72.

Morison, E. (1966), *Men, Machines and Modern Times.* Cambridge, MA and London: MIT Press.

Morris, P. (2013), Reconstructing Project Management (Wiley). Summarized latest book in an article for *Project Management Journal* 44 (5): 6–23.

Morris, P.W.G., Pinto, J.K., and Söderlund, J. (Eds.). (2011), *The Oxford Handbook of Project Management.* Oxford: Oxford University Press, pp. 15–36.

Moulton, H.G. (1910), The Manchester Ship Canal. *Journal of Political Economy*, 18 (6): 449–464.

Nicholls, R. (1996), *Trafford Park: The First Hundred Years.* Cheltenham: Phillimore & Co.

Oliver, A. (2008), Doug on the dig. Douglas Oakervee Interview. Building Crossrail: Major Project Report. *New Civil Engineer* November, 4–6.

Owen, D. (1983), *The Manchester Ship Canal.* Manchester: Manchester University Press, p. 53.

Piercy, N. (2012), Business History and Operations Management. *Business History* 54 (2): 154–178.

Pitagorsky, G. (2006), Agile and Lean Project Management: A Zen-Like Approach to Find Just the Right Degree of Formality for Your Project. Paper presented at PMI® Global Congress 2006—North America, Seattle, WA. Newtown Square, PA: Project Management Institute.

Reuters. (2018). Retrieved from https://www.reuters.com/article/uber-results/uber-narrows-loss-but-still-a-long-way-from-profitability-idUSL1N1V611I. Accessed February 4, 2019.

Rolt, L.T.C. (1984), *George and Robert Stephenson: The Railway Revolution*. London: Penguin.

Ryall, M.J. (2000), *The Manual of Bridge Engineering*. London: Thomas Telford.

Salerno et al. (2015), Innovation Processes: Which Process for Which Project? *Technovation* 35: 59–70.

Schadler, T., and Fenwick, N. (2017), Digital Rewrites: The Rules of Business, Vision: The Digital Business Transformation Playbook. Forrester.

Scholefield, R. (2004), *Manchester's Early Airfields—An Extensive Article in Moving Manchester*. Lancashire & Cheshire Antiquarian Society.

Scranton, P. (2010), *Projects as Business History: Surveying the Landscape*. New Brunswick, NJ: Rutgers University Press.

Scranton, P. (2014), Projects as a Focus for Historical Analysis: Surveying the Landscape. *History and Technology* 30 (4): 354–373. https://doi.org/10.1080/07341512.2014.1003164.

Sergeeva, N. (2017), Labeling Projects as Innovative: A Social Identity Theory. *Project Management Journal* 48 (1): 51–64.

Smiles, S. (1857), *The Life of George Stephenson and of His Son Robert Stephenson: Comprising Also a History of the Invention and Introduction of the Railway Locomotive*. New York, CA: Harper Brothers.

Smith, M. (1968), Ford of Britain: Yesterday Today.... *Autocar*. 128 (nbr 3766) (April 18): 52–54.

Snow, R. (1985), Herman Haupt. *American Heritage* 36 (2) (February/March): 54–55.

Söderlund, J., and Lenfle, S. (2011), Special Issue: Project History. *International Journal of Project Management* 29: 491–493.

Stake, R. (2005), Qualitative Case Studies. In N.K. Denzin and Y.S. Lincoln (Eds.), *The Sage Handbook of Qualitative Research* (3rd ed.). Thousand Oaks, CA: Sage, 443–466.

Stone, L. (1979), The Revival of Narrative: Reflections on a New Old History. *Past and Present* 85 (Nov 1979): 3–24, quote on p. 13 https://www.jstor.org/stable/650677?seq=1#page_scan_tab_contents.

Surowiecki, J. (2013), Where Nokia Went Wrong. *New Yorker*. Retrieved from https://www.newyorker.com/business/currency/where-nokia-went-wrong.

Taneja, H. (2019). Retrieved May 16, 2019, from https://hbr.org/2019/01/the-era-of-move-fast-and-break-things-is-over.

Taylor, F. (1911), *Principles of Scientific Management*. New York: Harper.

Tiersky, H. (2017), Navigating Digital Transformation. *CIO Magazine*. Retrieved from https://www.cio.com/article/3179607/e-commerce/5-top-challenges-to-digital-transformation-in-the-enterprise.html.

Tomlinson, William Weaver. (1915), *The North Eastern Railway: Its Rise and Development*. Newcastle upon Tyne: Andrew Reid & Co.

Waller, G., and Raskino, M. (2017), Master the Triple Tipping Point to Time Investments in Digital Business Strategy, Gartner; Foundational Refreshed: October 18, 2017; Published: February 9, 2016 ID: G00296107; Analyst(s): Graham P. Waller and Mark Raskino.

Willan, T. (1977), In W.H. Chaloner and Barrie M. Ratcliffe (Eds..), *Trade and Transport: Essays in Economic History in Honour of T. S. Willan*. Manchester University Press, ISBN 0-8476-6013-3.

Wrigley, A. (2018), Reconsidering the Industrial Revolution: England and Wales. *Journal of Interdisciplinary History* 49 (1): 9–42.

Gartner

Aronow et al. (2018), Gartner Supply Chain Top 25 for 2018; Published: May 16, 2018 ID: G00351344; Analyst(s): Stan Aronow, Kimberly Ennis, and Jim Romano.

Beresford, J., and Coelho, M. (2018), Scaling Enterprise Agility to Transform Established Organisations: BNP Paribas Fortis Bank, Gartner.

Bloom, B. (2019), Should Your View of the Customer Be Singular or Plural? March 25.

Burkett et al. (2017), Make Digital Business Transformation a Practical Reality: A Gartner Trend Insight Report, ID: G00332548; Published: October 27, 2017 ID: G00332548; Analyst(s): Michael Burkett and Patrick Meehan.

Burton et al. (2016), Every Organisation Needs a Digital Platform Strategy, ID: G00316151, Gartner.

Howard. (2017), High-Tech Manufacturing Supply Chainnovators 2016: Connecting, Collaborating and Capitalizing on Complexity, Gartner; Foundational Refreshed: October 18, 2017; Published: May 17, 2016 ID: G00307562; Analyst(s): Virginia Howard. https://www.gartner.com/en/products/special-reports.

Kopcho, J. (2018), A Program Office Is Crucial for Digital Transformation Program Success, Gartner; Published: December 18, 2018 ID: G00370314.

Kutnick, D. (2017), Exploit New Economic Models to Highlight Digital Business Contribution; Published: November 8, 2017 ID: G00335980; Analyst(s): Dale Kutnick, Patrick Meehan, Valentin Sribar, Chet Geschickter, and Irving Tyler.

LeHong, Waller. (2017), Digital Business Ambition: Transform or Optimise? Gartner; Published: June 30, 2017 ID: G00333254; Analyst(s): Hung LeHong and Graham P. Waller.

Morello, D. (2016), Five Steps to Build Your Digital Business Dream Team; Published: March 21, 2016; Analyst(s): Diane Morello.

Prentice, B. (2017), Digital Business Transformation Strategy Needs a Change of Perspective, Gartner; Published: September 12, 2017 ID: G00332711; Analyst(s): Brian Prentice.

Raskino, M. (2015), Fifty Examples of Digital Business: A CIO and CEO Resource, Gartner; Published: November 20, 2015 ID: G00278154; Analyst(s): Mark Raskino, Hung LeHong, and Don Scheibenreif.

Scott, D., Mingay, S., and Hotle, M. (2018), Leveraging Digital Product Management: A Gartner Trend Insight Report, Gartner; Published: November 16, 2018 ID: G00373974; Analyst(s): Donna Scott, Simon Mingay, and Matthew Hotle.

Swanton et al. (2017), A Digital Business Technology Platform Is Fundamental to Scaling Digital Business; Published: October 2, 2017 ID: G00342253; Analyst(s): Bill Swanton and Hung LeHong.

Waller. (2017), Master the Triple Tipping Point to Time Investments in Digital Business Strategy, Gartner; Foundational Refreshed: October 18, 2017; Published: February 9, 2016 ID: G00296107; Analyst(s): Graham P. Waller and Mark Raskino.

Wiles, J. (2018), Mobilize Every Function in the Organisation for Digitalization, Gartner.

No Author

'Trafford Park', n.d. Retrieved February 16, 2019, from http://lamptech.co.uk/Documents/Factory%20-%20UK%20-%20Trafford%20Park.htm.

'Ford at Trafford Park', 1911, n.d. Retrieved February 16 and January 21, 2019, from https://henryfordleadershiplegacy.weebly.com/short-term.html or https://www.sportscardigest.com/ford-of-britain-100th-anniversary-photo-gallery/2/.

'Transition vs Transformation—What's the Difference?', n.d. Wiki Article. Retrieved January 21, 2019, from https://wikidiff.com/transition/transformation.

'CPPR FAQ', n.d. CPRR Museum Article. Retrieved February 14, 2019, from https://cprr.org/Museum/FAQs.html.

'Black Powder and Nitroglycerine on the Transcontinental Railroad', n.d. Article. Retrieved February 14, 2019, from https://railroad.lindahall.org/essays/innovations.html.

'Snow Sheds: How the CPRR Crossed the Summit', n.d. Article. Retrieved February 14, 2019, from https://railroad.lindahall.org/essays/innovations.html.

'In Telegraph: Development of the Telegraph Industry', n.d. Britannica Article. Retrieved January 26, 2019, from https://www.britannica.com/technology/telegraph#ref607719.

'The Pacific Railroad Act of 1862 (12 Stat. 489) was the original act. Some of its provisions were subsequently modified, expanded, or repealed by four additional amending Acts: The Pacific Railroad Act of 1863 (12 Stat. 807), Pacific Railroad Act of 1864 (13 Stat. 356), Pacific Railroad Act of 1865 (13 Stat. 504), and Pacific Railroad Act of 1866 (14 Stat. 66)', n.d. Wiki Article. Retrieved September 6, 2018, from https://en.wikipedia.org/wiki/Pacific_Railroad_Acts.

'Facts and Figures, Manchester Ship Canal', archived from the original on 5 November 2007, n.d. (2007), Wiki. Retrieved October 1, 2007, from https://wikishire.co.uk/wiki/Barton_Swing_Aqueduct.

'Project Management Job Growth and Talent Gap Report 2017–2027', PMI, n.d. (2017).

'Top Strategic Predictions for 2019 and Beyond: Practicality Exists Within Instability', Gartner, n.d. (2018).

Index

M. Kozak-Holland and C. Procter, *Managing Transformation Projects*, https://doi.org/10.1007/978-3-030-33035-4

The manufacturer's authorised representative in the EU is Springer Nature Customer Service Centre GmbH, Europaplatz 3, 69115 Heidelberg, Germany. If you have any concerns regarding our products, please contact ProductSafety@springernature.com

Printed and bound by CPI Group (UK) Ltd, Croydon, CR0 4YY

30/09/2026

02225468-0002